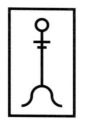

FAST PLANTS

CHOOSING AND GROWING PLANTS FOR GARDENS IN A HURRY

SUE FISHER

A Fireside Book
Published by Simon & Schuster
New York   London   Toronto   Sydney   Singapore

FIRESIDE
Rockefeller Center
1230 Avenue of the Americas
New York, NY 10020

Originally published in Great Britain in 2002 by
Collins & Brown Limited

Published by arrangement with Collins & Brown Limited

First Fireside Edition 2003

FIRESIDE and colophon are registered trademarks
of Simon & Schuster, Inc.

Designed by Liz Brown

Reproduction by Global Colour Separation Ltd, Malaysia
Printed and bound in Singapore by Imago

1 3 5 7 9 10 8 6 4 2

Library of Congress Cataloging-in-Publication Data
is available.

ISBN 0-7432-3317-4

For information about special discounts for bulk
purchases, please contact Simon & Schuster Special Sales:
1-800-456-6798 or business@simonandschuster.com

contents

Introduction

In today's fast-moving world, many people don't have the time to wait years for a garden to develop. Fast-growing plants are the answer to all sorts of difficult situations. Perhaps you have a brand-new garden that needs to be filled in a hurry; perhaps privacy or screening is desperately needed; or there may be unsightly objects to block out. Until now, the problem facing gardeners has been exactly which plants are the speediest growers out of the thousands available.

Now, for the very first time, the fastest-growing plants have been selected and brought together in one book. These plants are garden-worthy, too; they have been selected for their reliable performance and good looks, as well as for their speed of growth. There are plants for every situation around the garden: trees and large shrubs for planting alone; plants in all sizes for borders; shrubs and conifers for hedging; ground-covering plants for banks and borders; and climbers for walls, fences, or vertical features. Planning these key areas of the garden is explored in detail to help you combine your plants in the fastest, most effective way.

Apart from the permanent plants that are covered in detail in the Plant Directory, there are others that can be used to achieve a garden in a hurry. Certain groups of plants can all be classified as "fast," such as annuals and biennials that complete their life cycles within one or two growing seasons, and bulbs, which already contain their own source of energy and can begin growing without delay. And, for the truly instant garden, it is possible to "buy time" by purchasing ready-grown mature plants.

Choosing the right plants will lead you toward having a substantial garden in a short time, but how you prepare, plant, and care for your garden can make an enormous difference in growth rates. Therefore, this book also contains plenty of practical advice on how to get your plants sprinting off to a flying start and, with an eye to the future, how to keep any really speedy plants in check, too.

Quick ground cover *Transform bare soil into a colourful carpet of flowers and foliage with Serbian bellflower* (Campanula poscharskyana).

Rapid height *Tall perennials, such as* Verbena bonariensis, Echinacea purpurea *and* Galega officinalis, *create a great impact in a few months.*

PLANNING AND PLANTING

Permanent planting in beds and borders

Most garden plants are grown in beds and borders. Mixed borders are by far the best for achieving a "fast" garden that looks good year-round, yet which requires minimal maintenance. To create a mixed border, combine different types of plants such as trees, shrubs, conifers, and perennials. Choose flowering plants to give a succession of color through every season of the year, and include a fair proportion of evergreens and foliage plants for long-lasting structure and color. Fill the gaps with added dashes of seasonal flowers from bulbs and short-lived plants like annuals and biennials (see pages 30–39).

Putting all these plants together in the best combinations is one of the most challenging aspects of gardening. Check labels for eventual size, and place plants accordingly—with tall plants at the back of the border and medium to small ones graduating down to the front. While it is logical to plant like this for the most part, the occasional tall plant near the front enlivens a border tremendously, provided it is one like giant needle grass (*Stipa gigantea*) or Brazilian verbena (*Verbena bonariensis*) which has a light, airy texture. Place all plants so that their shapes contrast—for example, spiky plants next to rounded and carpet-forming ones—to give even more visual interest to the border. Be sure of the best combinations by standing plants on the ground in their pots and shuffling them

FAST EVERGREENS

Evergreens are invaluable for year-round structure and winter interest. Although most of these useful plants grow fairly slowly, the ones listed here are the fastest of the evergreens listed in the Plant Directory.

Boxleaf honeysuckle 'Baggesen's Gold'
California golden privet 'Aureum'
California lilac
Cider gum
Common cherry laurel
Ebbinge's silverberry
Escallonia 'Apple Blossom'
Leatherleaf viburnum
Laurustinus viburnum

around until you are satisfied with the final look. Then, and only then, get out your spade and start planting.

How far apart to plant is a question that frequently vexes gardeners. While it is incredibly tempting to create a fast garden by cramming plants close together, overplanting is a common trap that could lead to a lot of remedial work in a few years. The secret of success for both the short and long term is to space the long-lived, permanent plants well apart to allow for their eventual spread, and then to fill in between the permanent plants with short-lived plants and plants that won't mind being moved in future.

Where to start

Start with larger plants that will form the backbone of the garden, like trees, shrubs, conifers, and bamboos; place these key plants first, along with a few slower-growing evergreens that will make superb structural plants over time. Then, add several shrubs that live fast but die young, like broom (*Cytisus*) and tree mallow (*Lavatera*). Now, fill some of the spaces in between with plants that won't mind being moved, like small shrubs, ground-cover plants, herbaceous perennials, and ornamental grasses. These last two actually benefit from being lifted, divided, and replanted after around 4 to 5 years, once they have formed large, established clumps, so moving them later on is no problem at all. Finally, fill the remaining gaps with short-lived seasonal flowers like annuals, frost-tender perennials, and biennials, which are wonderful for spring and summer color.

Whichever part of the garden is to be planted, by far the most important consideration is to choose plants that like the conditions to be found at that site. Happy plants that feel at home will grow quickly and look good, while plants in the wrong place will sulk and fail to thrive. For all the necessary practical information, see the section starting on page 20.

Mixed borders *Create a well-filled look in borders by cramming the spaces between larger plants with fast perennials like lady's mantle* (Alchemilla mollis) *that are happy to be moved later on.*

Climbers on walls, fences, and vertical features

Because of their tremendous versatility, climbing plants offer the greatest opportunities for rapidly exploiting the potential of every garden. Adapting themselves to whatever support is provided, climbing plants quickly scramble upward and establish themselves in a short amount of time. Climbers offer a tremendously high ratio of plant growth to ground occupancy, as well, making them the perfect choice where space is limited.

The greatest instant impact can be created by constructing vertical features such as arches, arbors, pergolas, and obelisks, all of which can be tailored to fit any size garden. These structures add a whole new dimension to the garden in their own right, even before the climbing plants get going. Arbors and pergolas are perfect to sit beneath and be sheltered from excess sun and wind; arches and tunnels are ideal for dividing different areas of the garden and are a delight to walk through; screens made of trellis or other materials divide up the garden and can rapidly be clothed with climbers; while free-standing supports for climbing plants can be dropped into borders to make "exclamation marks" of instant height.

Walls and fences are ready-made sites that are ideal for planting with a wide range of climbers. Such sites are also suitable for wall shrubs—plants that can be closely trained against a vertical surface—provided they are tied in regularly and pruned once or twice a year. Most climbers and all wall shrubs need some form of support such as trellis, wire mesh, or strong galvanized wires.

The permanent climbers in the Plant Directory (see box,) are excellent for rapid cover; in addition, there are also annual climbers (see page 36) that are incredibly useful for providing color for a single season. Plan for the longer term by planting a percentage of evergreen climbers such as Persian ivy (*Hedera colchica*), English ivy (*H. helix*), tanglehead (*Pileostegia viburnoides*), evergreen laburnum (*Piptanthus nepalensis*), firethorn (*Pyracantha*), and *Trachelospermum*. Climbing roses grow fast once established but generally take a year or two to settle in before starting to grow strongly.

Vertical features *An obelisk swathed in sweet peas* (Lathyrus odoratus) *makes an instant impact.*

Speedy climbers *Bluecrown passionflower* (Passiflora caerulea) *soon covers all sorts of structures and creates an air of permanence.*

FAST CLIMBERS AND WALL SHRUBS

Bluecrown passionflower
Bukhara fleeceflower
California flannelbush
California lilac
Cape fuchsia
Chilean glory flower
Chilean potato tree 'Glasnevin'
Clematis (all hybrids and species listed)
European honeysuckle
Five-leaf akebia
Jasmine
Silver-vein creeper
Trumpet creeper
Winter jasmine

Creating shelter and privacy

Sometimes the need for fast plants is a purely practical one. Perhaps privacy is badly needed, either from neighboring houses or from passers-by; there may be unsightly objects that need screening within the garden or yard; or perhaps shelter from excess sun or wind is needed in order to enjoy the garden to the fullest.

For instant effect, use climbing plants on some sort of support. A screen of trellis or similar material can be put up almost anywhere and in itself creates a certain degree of shelter and privacy; but clothed with climbers, it becomes a living and colorful feature that can transform your garden. In a windy situation, an open screen is usually a better option than a solid barrier, as the wind can filter through, rather than creating turbulence on the lee side of a solid fence. Good, fast, permanent plants for growing on screens are all types of clematis (*Clematis*), Chilean glory flower (*Eccremocarpus scaber*), jasmine (*Jasminum officinale*), European honeysuckle (*Lonicera periclymenum*), and bluecrown passionflower (*Passiflora caerulea*). Annual climbers (see page 36) do a great job of filling any gaps for the summer.

A pergola over a patio can be amazingly effective in creating privacy from neighboring upstairs windows, and the sides can also be filled in with trellis if extra screening is required. All the climbers listed above are suitable for pergolas, as well as chocolate vine (*Akebia*) and trumpet creeper (*Campsis*), in mild areas. Hedges make superb living screens, and they become more beautiful with the passage of time compared to man-made barriers, which deteriorate. But even the fastest-growing hedge takes several years to provide a good degree of privacy. Where complete privacy is essential, plant a hedge and then put up a fence or screen and leave it in place for 3 to 4 years until the hedge is well established. As a bonus, the hedge will grow faster in the sheltered environment made by the fence. Where a hedge is planted by itself, it is an excellent idea to put up a temporary shelter of windbreak netting for the first year or two.

Choose between a neatly trimmed, formal hedge, which will need pruning two or even three times a year, or an informal hedge, which only needs pruning once a year, if necessary, but which occupies more space as a result. Fast shrubs and conifers for formal hedges are Lawson false cypress (*Chamaecyparis lawsoniana*), Leyland cypress (× *Cupressocyparis leylandii*), California golden privet (*Ligustrum ovalifolium* 'Aureum'), and Western red cedar (*Thuja plicata* 'Atrovirens'). Shrubs for informal hedges include common cherry laurel (*Prunus laurocerasus*), cinquefoil (*Potentilla* 'Katherine Dykes'), winter currant (*Ribes sanguineum*), rugosa rose (*Rosa rugosa*), coralberry (*Symphoricarpos*), and laurustinus viburnum (*Viburnum tinus*). For coastal areas, escallonia (*Escallonia*) and salt cedar (*Tamarix tetrandra*) make good hedges.

Sometimes privacy is only required in certain places—where a neighboring window overlooks the garden, for example—and an entire hedge or screen is not necessary. "Spot" screening – using tall plants alone or in small groups—may be the answer here. The conifers and tall shrubs listed above are ideal for spot screening, as are bamboos (*Chusquea culeou* and *Phyllostachys*) and trees such as European white birch (*Betula pendula*), crab apple (*Malus*), and double mazzard cherry (*Prunus avium* 'Plena'). If planting in groups, always use odd numbers of plants for a harmonious appearance, unless the design is a formal one.

Living screens *Fast-growing hedging plants are vital to create valuable shelter and privacy in a relatively short time.*

FAST SCENTED FLOWERS

Anemone clematis (some cultivars)
Broom
Buddleja
Chinese loquat
Ebbinge's silverberry
European honeysuckle
Five-leaf akebia
Jasmine
Lavender
Mexican orange flower
Mock orange
Rose (some)
Spanish broom

Quick ground cover for beds and banks

Areas of bare ground can be transformed with a carpet of low-growing plants that create a tapestry of color right through the year. Apart from the improvement in aesthetics, bare soil is a prime target for weeds, which, if allowed to establish and set seed, will be a dreadful nuisance to clear. Banks that are left unplanted are susceptible to a more serious problem—soil erosion by wind and rain.

The most dramatic and attractive effects are created by using a limited number of plant varieties in bold groups so that the planting looks good whether seen close up or from a distance. Use odd numbers of plants—groupings of three, five, or seven plants, and so on—in an informal design and even numbers in a formal one. In order to have something of interest all year, choose a mixture of deciduous and evergreen plants, and stagger flowering times so there is color in every season.

To get the maximum amount of color and interest from the garden, use shade-tolerant ground-cover plants to go under trees and large shrubs. The following plants will thrive in all but

Dense ground cover *Blue catmint (Nepeta × faassenii) is an excellent ground-cover plant that is popular for its fast growth and aromatic foliage.*

dense shade: lady's mantle (*Alchemilla mollis*), bergenia (*Bergenia*), Serbian bellflower (*Campanula poscharskyana*), Welsh poppy (*Meconopsis cambrica*), Himalayan fleeceflower (*Persicaria affinis*), and large variegated periwinkle (*Vinca major* 'Variegata'). Speedwell (*Veronica peduncularis* 'Georgia Blue') prefers sun or part shade. All of these plants are tolerant of most soils, while hosta (*Hosta sieboldiana* 'Elegans') loves shade but must not be allowed to dry out.

All of the plants listed above (except the hosta) are happy in full sun; but there are others that are real sun-worshippers—they detest the shade—notably gray- or silver-leafed plants and those with hairy foliage. These include horehound (*Ballota*), juniper (*Juniperus*), blue catmint (*Nepeta × faassenii*), and purple sage (*Salvia officinalis* 'Purpurascens').

If there is a large area of space in your garden that is to be covered solely with ground-cover plants, opt for really vigorous varieties that will rapidly create a very dense carpet of foliage and flowers. Two of the most vigorous spreaders are Himalayan fleeceflower, large

FAST PLANTS FOR DRY BANKS AND BORDERS

Ballota
Blue catmint
Brachyglottis
Broom
California flannelbush
California lilac
Chilean glory flower
Giant needle grass
Hellebore
Juniper
Lavender cotton
Mullein
Rock rose
Russian sage
Sage
Spanish broom
Wallflower
Wormwood

Shady and sunny sites *The colonizing tendencies of the Welsh poppy* (Meconopsis cambrica) *make it invaluable ground cover for shady and sunny sites.*

variegated periwinkle, and the Gamebird series of roses (*Rosa*).

These vigorous varieties are excellent for use on slopes to stabilize the soil—large variegated periwinkle is outstanding for this purpose, because its shoots arch over and root where they touch the ground, quickly creating many new plants. Serbian bellflower is also good for stabilizing soil, spreading by means of underground runners. If the soil is very unstable, it is a good idea to use planting membrane, which is a woven material that suppresses weeds but lets water through. Lay the membrane over the soil and cut an x-shaped hole through which to put each plant. Although the membrane will look unsightly for the first year or two, the plant growth will soon spread to conceal it.

FAST PLANTS FOR BORDERS WITH MOISTURE-RETENTIVE SOIL

Cherry
Cinquefoil
Crab apple
Dogwood
Kerria
Maple
Mexican orange flower
Mock orange
Periwinkle
Snowberry
Spiraea
St.-John's-wort
Tibetan bramble
Willow
Winter currant
Viburnum
Weigela

Short cuts to instant gardens

Where even the fastest plants may not be quick enough, it is possible to create a garden that is truly instant. Mature shrubs, conifers, and climbers—usually referred to as specimens—can be bought from garden centers or direct from nurseries, while herbaceous perennials are also available as decent-sized plants. Once all danger of frost has passed, there are many frost-tender annuals and perennials (see page 36) that can be bought as ready-grown plants and planted closely together for immediate impact.

Mature and specimen plants

Mature permanent plants are grown in nurseries for a number of years and therefore are expensive; it is worth choosing with care to be sure you are spending your money wisely. For starters, a good rule of thumb is to avoid almost all the plants listed in this book; these are not good values when bought as mature specimens, because they quickly achieve a decent size when planted young. Two exceptions are bamboo and tree ferns (*Dicksonia antarctica*), which are outstanding for architectural effect and are well worth buying in larger sizes.

Choose specimen plants that will give your garden year-round structure and style, but which will take a fair amount of time to reach a reasonable size. Look for evergreens and slower-growing conifers; plants that have been trimmed into topiary shapes; slower-growing deciduous shrubs like Japanese maple (*Acer palmatum*); and shrubs like magnolia (*Magnolia*) that only begin to flower profusely when several years old.

If money is no object, you can buy mature plants in incredibly large sizes. Speciality landscaping companies can supply huge trees and substantial shrubs that need to be planted with the aid of heavy-lifting machines. Such plants are grown in nursery fields for many years and are undercut regularly, producing compact rootballs that can be transplanted easily.

If you live in a cold area and are considering buying a mature plant, be sure to check into the nursery's supplier – a good deal of stock is bought from nurseries in warm countries where growth rates are very fast. As a result, plants may take a while to acclimatize to local conditions; therefore, it is best to buy and plant mature plants in spring or early summer in order for

them to become well established before winter. Even then, protect the plants with fleece or netting for the first winter or two. In the first two years, be sure to water all mature plants thoroughly during dry spells.

Perennials and grasses

Herbaceous perennials and ornamental grasses can be bought in different sizes. While even the smallest plants can create a reasonable display in their first year if planted close together, large plants are excellent for immediate effect. In most cases, perennials and grasses look best when planted fairly close together in groups of three or five of one variety. Large plants are a good investment, not only for their immediate impact, but also for providing stock for the future. Once perennials or grasses are around 4 to 5 years old, they actually benefit from being lifted, divided into smaller clumps, and replanted. In a new garden, it makes sense to buy substantial plants for high-profile areas around the house and patio, because after a year or two they can be divided to provide stock for elsewhere in the garden. Sometimes it is even possible to buy plants in 5- or 10-liter pots, though the increase in price is quite substantial compared with the amount of growing time you will save.

Large specimen plants *Be sure to spend your money wisely and choose varieties like Japanese maples which are sumptuous yet slow-growing.*

Tree fern *It is well worth buying a large specimen, as its trunk grows just 12in (30cm) in ten years.*

PREPARATION AND CULTIVATION

Preparing the ground

The speed at which a plant grows can be greatly influenced by good ground preparation, planting, and aftercare. This 'nuts and bolts' aspect of gardening may not sound exciting, but it is necessary if you want to get the fastest possible growth from your plants.

Different plants have varying preferences as to their growing conditions, so it really does pay dividends to do a bit of research on your plot before choosing any plants at all. While there are a few easy-going plants that tolerate most conditions, the vast majority are particular about site to some extent. Bear in mind that a plant growing in ideal conditions will grow faster, be more vigorous, and perform much better than a plant growing in the wrong place. The most important considerations are orientation, which is the amount of sun or shade a site receives, and soil type, along with the soil's level of acidity or alkalinity.

TESTING SOIL pH

(1) The pH of your soil can be determined using a simple pH testing kit. Set out canes in a "W" shape and take a small sample of soil from each point. As pH levels can vary, test each bed or area separately.

(2) In a shallow dish, crumble the soil between your fingers and mix it thoroughly. Remove any stones or other debris.

(3) Place a small amount of the mixed soil in the test tube to the level specified. Following the test kit instructions, fill the tube with pH test fluid and shake well.

(4) Leave the test tube to settle for a few minutes and then compare the colour of the liquid in the top part of the tube with the colour chart supplied with the testing kit.

Mulching *Good soil preparation will pay dividends in terms of rapid plant growth. Hostas are particularly appreciative of a thick mulch.*

working in organic matter to one spade's depth is sufficient. However, ground that is in poor condition or with little topsoil really needs organic matter worked in to two spades' depths, a technique called double digging. To do this, first dig out a trench and put the soil to one side. Then, use a spading fork to dig over the soil in the base of the trench as deeply as possible, and work in lots of organic matter. Dig a second trench and use that soil to fill the first trench. Repeat over the whole area and fill in the last trench with the soil from the first one.

Heavy soils are best dug in autumn and left rough in large clods over winter for the frost to break down. While this sounds like a lot of hard work—and it is!—remember that you'll only be able to work the ground this thoroughly before any planting is done. You and your plants will reap the benefits for years.

Organic matter comes in many forms. Composted bark and concentrated animal manure are sold in bags, and while convenient and easy to handle, they can be expensive if you are preparing a large area of ground. Save money by buying unbagged material in bulk, or opt for cheaper alternatives like horse or farmyard manure—which must be at least six months old—or spent mushroom compost. Set up a couple of compost bins, as well, and recycle your garden and kitchen waste.

Soil type

Soil varies enormously from place to place, both in pH—the level of acidity or alkalinity—and in type. To determine your soil's pH quickly and easily, buy a simple test kit – it is always worth doing. Take a soil sample dug from around 6 in (15cm) deep, from ground that has not been contaminated by imported topsoil.

Soil type affects whether the ground drains freely or retains moisture. Soils that are predominantly sandy, stony, or chalky are made up of large particles that allow water to drain away quickly, whereas clay and silt contain tiny particles that hold water well. The ideal soil – loam – is made up of a combination of large and small particles; it can be created over time by incorporating plenty of organic matter into your soil, both before planting and then as a mulch each year.

Improving your soil

Improving the soil by adding organic matter is always worth doing. Light, free-draining soils need it to improve their capacity to hold water and nutrients, while heavy ones such as clay and silt need organic matter to open out their structure and improve drainage. In most cases,

Weeding

Thoroughly clear weeds from the soil, or they'll compete with your plants for water and nutrients, thereby reducing your plants' growth rates. Annual weeds—those that complete their life cycle in one year—are a nuisance rather than a problem, as they are easily wiped out by hoeing or hand-weeding. Perennial weeds are a different matter—they regrow from even a tiny piece of root left in the soil and must be cleared by thorough digging or by spraying with a systemic (translocated) weedkiller while they are actively growing. Take care to keep weedkiller away from garden plants as it will kill any growth that it touches.

Planting and cultivating

Planting

The quality of planting and aftercare makes the difference between a plant that sprints off the starting blocks and one that is left at the gate to build up momentum gradually. With a bit of attention to detail at the planting stage and no shortage of water during the first year, a plant should begin growing quickly and without delay.

To give plants a really good start in life, use compost. Made up of a fine grade of organic matter plus enough fertilizer for the first season, compost often contains water-retaining granules that provide a reservoir of moisture during dry spells. Mixed into the planting hole and the excavated soil, it encourages roots to grow outward into the harsher environment of the garden soil.

Before planting, give a plant's roots a good soaking by standing the plant in a bucket of water for an hour or so. Remove the plant from its pot, loosening it if necessary by holding the pot upside-down and gently tapping it against a hard surface. If there are a lot of roots spiralling around the bottom of the rootball, gently tease them loose. Inspect bare-rooted plants and trim off any damaged roots.

Put the plant in a hole slightly larger than the rootball so the top of the rootball is level with the ground (the only exception is clematis, which does best when planted about 4in (10cm) below ground). Backfill around the roots with soil, and firm the soil gently with your heel. Create a saucer-shaped depression in the soil around the base, so water will gather there to soak down to the roots. Always water thoroughly immediately after planting.

Mulching the bare soil around plants with a 2 to 4-in (5 to 10-cm) layer of material such as chipped bark will give a huge boost to plant establishment and growth rates, and will reduce maintenance, as well. Mulch cuts down on the amount of water that evaporates from the soil, stops the majority of weeds from growing and helps to prevent roots from becoming too hot or too cold. Apply mulch only when the soil is wet, because dry ground will be hard to soak afterward. To avoid getting mulch near the centers of small plants, which can cause rotting, protect them by covering them with overturned pots or buckets and keep them clear of plant stems.

PLANTING A PLANT

1 Dig out a hole slightly deeper and wider than the plant's pot or rootball. Mix some planting compost into the hole and the excavated soil.

2 Take the plant out of its pot. If the roots are spiralling around the rootball, use your fingers or a stick to tease some of them out.

3 Put the plant in the hole so the top of the rootball is level with the ground (lay a stick or bamboo cane across the top to check the levels) then backfill the gap with soil. Firm the soil gently with your heel and water the plant well.

Watering and feeding

In the first year after planting, watering during dry spells is crucial to success, because the plant will not have established a good root system yet. Take care to give the roots a good soaking, because a little water is worse than none at all – light watering encourages the roots to grow upward in search of what little moisture there is.

Plastic bottles provide a simple, cost-free way to take water straight to where it is needed. When planting, before you backfill with soil, take a cut-down plastic bottle (see right) and sink it upside-down into the ground, filling around it with soil so that only a little bit is visible. Then, by filling up the bottle at every watering, you can be sure the water goes directly to the roots. Large plants may need two or three bottles around the rootball.

A watering system is an excellent investment if you are frequently away from home. Use porous pipes for entire new borders, or use pipes fitted with individual drippers if your plants are spaced well apart or are in containers. Sprinklers waste a lot of water and should be avoided, if possible. A watering system can be fitted with a timer, making it fully automatic – in addition to coming in handy when you are away from home, a timer enables you to water plants in the early morning or evening, when less water will be lost to evaporation.

After several months, once the fertilizer in your compost has been exhausted, feeding becomes necessary. Because many plants growing in a limited amount of space take more out of the soil than they give back naturally, they will need to be fed with fertilizer at least a couple of times per year. It is important not to confuse fertilizers – which are plant foods in concentrated form – with soil improvers like manure and garden compost. Soil improvers do contain some nutrients, but not enough to keep your plants sufficiently well fed.

Garden plants should be fed in spring and summer, when they are growing strongly, using slow-release or controlled-release fertilizers. Apply fertilizer when the ground is moist but plants are dry, because fertilizer can stick to and scorch damp leaves. Keep the soil in good condition by mulching every spring with compost and manure as described on page 24.

USING A CUT-DOWN BOTTLE

1 Plastic bottles can be used to ensure plants are watered effectively. Take a large, empty plastic bottle 1.5 or 2 litres in size, remove the top and cut off the bottom.

2 Whilst planting and before backfilling with soil, put the bottle upside-down in the ground next to the rootball, so the rim is just above soil level.

3 Backfill with soil all around the rootball, leaving the edge of the bottle just visible. When watering the plant, fill the bottle right up and the water will go directly to the roots.

Pruning and training

Pruning

Pruning is rarely as tricky as it first appears. Indeed, for a couple of years after planting a garden, there will be very little regular pruning required apart from a few plants that need to be cut back every year. But as plants begin to mature and jostle with each other for space, you will need to break out the pruning tools and intervene. In the confines of a garden, plants need to be managed to ensure that they keep looking good.

Tools

There are plenty of different pruning tools to add to the gardener's armoury. However, unless you're inherited an overgrown jungle, it's unlikely that you will need to have all the ones featured below. The essential ones for maintaining any garden are a good pair of secateurs, a small pruning saw, and a pair of shears which also do duty for other jobs like trimming lawn edges. The choice of others depends on the type of plants that you have in your garden.

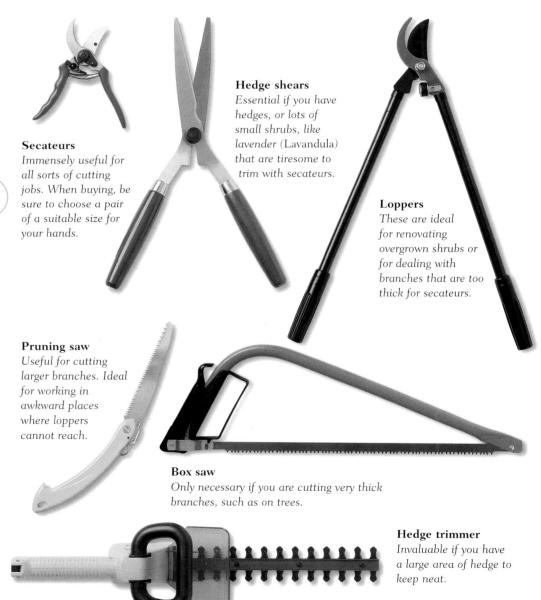

Secateurs
Immensely useful for all sorts of cutting jobs. When buying, be sure to choose a pair of a suitable size for your hands.

Hedge shears
Essential if you have hedges, or lots of small shrubs, like lavender (Lavandula) that are tiresome to trim with secateurs.

Loppers
These are ideal for renovating overgrown shrubs or for dealing with branches that are too thick for secateurs.

Pruning saw
Useful for cutting larger branches. Ideal for working in awkward places where loppers cannot reach.

Box saw
Only necessary if you are cutting very thick branches, such as on trees.

Hedge trimmer
Invaluable if you have a large area of hedge to keep neat.

The aims of pruning

The size and vigor of most plants can be controlled by regular pruning. It can also considerably extend a plant's life by encouraging fresh, productive growth over a longer period of time, rather than if it were to be left unpruned. One of the main aims of pruning is to let light and air to all parts of the plant, which will improve its overall growth.

From an aesthetic point of view, the shape of a plant can often be improved to make it more pleasing. Where space is limited, plants can be pruned to create maximum growing room; for example, by removing the lower branches of a large shrub so that there is space for low-growing plants underneath.

When to prune

Timing is everything; if you go on a pruning blitz at the wrong time of year, you could be unwittingly hacking off a whole crop of bloom. If you have inherited a garden and are unfamiliar with some of the plants, delay pruning until you can establish the plants' identities. A list of the major groups of plants that need annual pruning follows.

Deciduous shrubs that flower from mid-summer onwards

Cut back hard in early spring to within 2in (5cm) of last year's growth. By looking closely at the shoots, it is possible to see a definite difference between this year's slender, smooth-barked shoots and last year's thicker stems with darker, more weathered bark. This group includes butterfly bush (*Buddleja*), fuchsia (*Fuchsia*), tree mallow (*Lavatera*), and elderberry (*Sambucus*). Shrubs with colored stems like dogwood (*Cornus*) and willow (*Salix*) should be treated the same way.

Deciduous shrubs that flower from spring to early summer

Prune immediately after flowering has finished, cutting back all the shoots that have borne flowers. This group includes *Forsythia*, lavender, mock orange blossom (*Philadelphus*) and *Weigela*.

Renovating an overgrown deciduous shrub

If not pruned regularly, older shrubs have a tendency to become woody and bare in the middle. Most respond well to drastic pruning done over several years during late winter to early spring. Using a pruning saw, cut about one-third of the thickest, oldest branches, staying as close to ground level as possible. Cut out dead, diseased, and damaged wood. Thin any stems that are crossing and rubbing each other, as wounds allow diseases to enter. New shoots will grow from the base, and these should be thinned if overcrowded. Repeat the process over the next two years until all the oldest shoots have been removed.

How to prune deciduous shrubs that flower spring to early summer
Cut back all the shoots that have borne flowers, as indicated. Some shoots can be left unpruned to increase the size of the bush if desired.

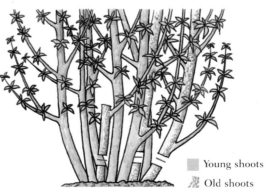

Young shoots
Old shoots

Pruning to renovate an overgrown deciduous shrub.
Cut out about a third of the oldest, thickest branches as close to the ground as possible. Repeat this process over the next two years.

Sharing a trellis *Climbing plants and wall shrubs really benefit from attention little and often, particularly when sharing a trellis with other plants.*

Evergreen shrubs

Most evergreen shrubs can be left to their own devices. Every spring, take a good look at each shrub and cut out any straggly shoots that are spoiling the shape of the plant. Tackle overgrown evergreens in midspring by removing several large branches as close to the ground as possible, which encourages new growth to come from the base and gives room for the remainder to spread out.

Roses

Prune roses in early spring. For shrub roses that are several years old, remove about one-third of the oldest branches closest to the ground. The ground-covering Gamebird roses can be cut back as necessary, and precision is not important; so much so that a brushcutter can be used to hack these plants back.

Climbers and wall shrubs

Plants growing on walls, fences, and upright features like pergolas, arches, and obelisks benefit from frequent attention. If neglected, climbing plants can quickly form a mass of tangled stems. Every couple of weeks, separate out shoots and encourage them to grow in the right direction. Tie in if necessary using soft string or twine, but do not use wire as it can cut into and damage stems. Wall shrubs need to be tied in regularly and pruned once or twice a year.

How climbers climb

Identifying the habit of a particular plant is immensely useful in partnering it to the best feature or support. There are three main ways in which plants climb.

Self-clinging climbers secure themselves by means of aerial roots or suckers on their stems, and include silver-vein creeper (*Parthenocissus henryana*) and ivy (*Hedera*). In the first year or two they benefit from a little training in the right direction until they are firmly attached. Avoid growing such plants on fences or on old walls with crumbling mortar, as they could cause damage.

Twining climbers have stems that spiral upwards and need to be grown on vertical or fan-shaped wires, or on trellis. This group includes five-leaf akebia (*Akebia quinata*) and European honeysuckle (*Lonicera periclymenum*).

Plants that climb by means of tendrils or twining leaf stalks need closely-spaced trellis, mesh or wires up which to scramble. This group of climbers includes *Clematis*, Chilean glory flower (*Eccremocarpus scaber*) and bluecrown passionflower (*Passiflora caerulea*).

PUTTING UP SUPPORTS

① Prepare the wooden battens by drilling screw holes at 18in (46cm) intervals. Hold a wooden batten against the wall, having first used a spirit level to check it is vertical, and knock nails through to mark the screw positions.

Supporting climbing plants

When grown on walls and fences, all plants, except for the self-clinging silver-vein creeper (*Parthenocissus henryana*), need some form of support, such as trellis or strong galvanized wire. Trellis is best for a small area and for a high-profile spot where the support, as well as the plant, needs to look good. Wire is cheap, long-lasting, and the best option for covering a large area of wall or fence.

Put up trellis using wooden battens to create a gap of at least 1 to 2in (2.5 to 5cm) so plants have room to twine. Strong galvanized wire needs to be run though vine eyes, which are screws with a metal loop at one end. Drill holes for vine eyes about every 6 feet (1.8m) in a row and with 9 to 12in (23 to 30.5cm) between each row. On walls, use plastic wall plugs and run the wires close to the lines of mortar so they will be hidden.

Trellis that is to be fixed to a solid wall or fence needs to be put up with wooden battens to create a gap of at least 1 to 2in (2.5 to 5cm). This gives sufficient room for stems to twine around the bars of the trellis, and allows for good air movement around the plant which helps discourage potential disease problems.

② Drill holes at the positions on the wall that you have marked for the screws and insert wall plugs into them. Screw the battens firmly to the wall.

③ Once the wooden battens are in place, screw the trellis firmly to the battens, using a spirit level to make sure that the trellis is positioned correctly.

Seasonal flowers

Late spring to early autumn is a wonderful time for some really fast gardening – there are many short-lived, seasonal plants that can be bursting with bloom in as little as a few weeks. Half-hardy annuals and tender perennials flower continuously from early summer until they are killed by the first hard frosts, while hardy annuals and biennials make a fantastic display of bloom for up to a couple of months. Use these versatile plants to make an entire border, to fill any gaps within a newly planted border, or to use in all kinds of containers to make a magical, movable display.

With an eye toward the long term, these plants make such a reliable show of summer flowers that it is well worth designating a few spots within borders for their use every year. Bulbs are excellent gap-fillers too, with the added bonus that most varieties will pop up year after year, making a superb show of flowers for a few weeks at a time.

Annuals and bulbs *White love-in-a-mist* (Nigella) *and feverfew* (Tanacetum) *rub shoulders with the dramatic blooms of* Allium cristophii.

FAST RESULTS WITH SEASONAL FLOWERS

	Hardy annuals, half-hardy annuals, tender perennials, biennials, and bulbs
Flowers in spring	Biennials—double daisy (*Bellis perennis*), forget-me-not (*Myosotis*), polyanthus (*Primula* 'Polyanthus Group'), wallflower (*Erysimum cheiri*) Bulbs—many, including glory-of-the-snow (*Chionodoxa*), crocus, hyacinths, narcissi, tulips
Flowers in summer	Biennials—foxglove (*Digitalis*), sweet rocket or dame's violet (*Hesperis matronalis*), sweet william (*Dianthus barbatus*) Bulbs—lilies (many varieties), ornamental onion (*Allium* species), gladioli Half-hardy annuals—many, including ageratum, busy lizzie (*Impatiens*), cosmos, morning glory (*Ipomoea*), lobelia, spider flower (*Cleome*), tobacco plant (*Nicotiana*) Hardy annuals—many, including clarkia, godetia, love-in-a-mist (*Nigella*), pot marigold (*Calendula*), nasturtium (*Tropaeolum majus*), sweet pea (*Lathyrus odoratus*), sunflower (*Helianthus annuus*) Tender perennials—many, including African daisy (*Osteospermum, Gazania*), monkey flower (*Mimulus aurantiacus*), *Diascia, Felicia amelloides,* marguerite daisy (*Argyranthemum*)
Flowers in autumn	Half-hardy annuals and tender perennials—as for summer, with the addition of chrysanthemums Hardy annuals—sown in mid-summer will bloom in autumn. Dahlias (tubers) are excellent for late-summer and autumn flowers
Flowers in winter	Bulbs—snowdrops (*Galanthus*) and winter aconites (*Eranthis hyemalis*)

Sowing hardy annuals

If you've never grown anything from seed before, start with hardy annuals. There's no need for any special equipment as seed can be sown straight into the ground, and most varieties are really easy to grow.

Hardy annuals are absolutely great for new gardens as they can be used to fill the gaps between newly-planted permanent plants, as well as looking fantastic in a border on their own. Sow them outside where they are to flower, either in autumn if the soil is well-drained or in spring if the soil is heavy.

PLANTING SEEDS

1 Choose a sunny spot for your border. First dig over the soil and rake it to break up any lumps, incorporating a general fertilizer at the same time.

2 Annuals look best when they're growing in irregularly-shaped patches. It's a good idea to clearly mark them by sprinkling sand or flour along the edges.

3 Within each patch, use a bamboo cane to draw out several shallow lines known as seed drills, about ½in (1cm) deep. Sowing seed in lines will make it easy to see the difference between young plants and weeds later on.

4 Sow the seed thinly in the drills. Rake a little soil over the seed and firm gently with the back of the rake.

5 When the seedlings have appeared, thin them out to leave approximately 3–4in (8–10cm) between each one.

Hardy annuals

Easy and quick to grow, hardy annuals produce masses of flowers within two to three months of the seed being sown. Although the blooms will not last as long as those of half-hardy annuals and tender perennials, you will still have a good couple of months of color for comparatively little money and effort. Hardy annuals are great plants for the starter gardener, as the seed is cheap to buy and can be grown outside without using any special equipment.

As their name suggests, hardy annuals tolerate frost and therefore can be sown outside in autumn or spring. Sow seed in autumn if the soil is well drained and the climate is not too cold; or sow in mid-spring to early summer in very cold areas, or if the soil is heavy and liable to become waterlogged in winter. Choose a sunny spot and

Annual climbers *Sweet peas (Lathyrus odoratus) are just one of many climbers that can cover all sorts of supports in the space of a few weeks.*

dig over and rake the ground, incorporating some general fertilizer. Mark out irregularly-shaped patches where each variety will be sown, and within each patch, draw out several shallow lines about ½in (1cm) deep.

Although seed can be sown broadcast, sowing in lines will make it easy to differentiate between plant and weed seedlings later on. Sow the seed thinly, rake a little soil over the top, and firm gently with the back of the rake. Once the seedlings are growing strongly, thin the plants to 4in (10cm) apart. Alternatively, seed can be sown under cover without heat, in pots or modular trays, for planting out in spring.

While there is an excellent range of plants to choose from, the following ones can usually be relied upon to produce a good show of bloom on reasonably-sized plants: Corn cockle (*Agrostemma*); pot marigold (*Calendula*); cornflower (*Centaurea cyanus*); annual varieties of chrysanthemum (*Chrysanthemum*); godetia (*Clarkia*); California poppy (*Eschscholzia*); sunflower (*Helianthus*); strawflower (*Helichrysum*); tree mallow (*Lavatera*); alyssum (*Lobularia maritima*); love-in-a-mist (*Nigella*); common nasturtium (*Tropaeolum majus*); and sweet pea (*Lathyrus odoratus*).

Half-hardy annuals & tender perennials

Nothing beats a riot of flowers all throughout the summer, just when you are most likely to be outside enjoying your garden to the fullest. These frost-tender plants are virtually guaranteed to put on a fantastic show for months on end, blooming from early to mid-summer until brought to an abrupt end by the first autumn frosts. While the vast majority are sun-lovers, a few do thrive in shade, such as impatiens (*Impatiens*), fuchsia, and lobelia (*Lobelia*).

Although these plants give excellent summer displays, certain varieties grow to an impressive size and are outstanding for creating a handsome display in a very short time. The most striking seed-raised annuals include flowering tobacco (*Nicotiana sylvestris*), which grows to around 5ft (1.5m) high with tubular, pure white flowers borne in tall "candelabras" on stout stems clad with huge, oval leaves. The blooms open in succession, so the display lasts for many weeks. Tall varieties of garden cosmos (*Cosmos bipinnatus*) reach up to 4ft (1.2m) by late summer and bear numerous large "daisy" flowers above attractive, feathery foliage. Spider flower (*Cleome hassleriana*), with its whiskered, white or pink blooms, grows to a similar height and makes an impressive display when planted in groups. The castor plant (*Ricinus communis*) has clusters of rounded, spiky, dark red flowers, but its main feature is its striking palmate, purple-green leaves.

Many tender perennials and shrubs soon reach a substantial size, as well. Marguerite daisy (*Argyranthemum foeniculaceum*) quickly forms

rounded bushes of feathery foliage up to 3ft (90cm) high covered with many "daisy" flowers in a wide range of colors, including white, pink, yellow, and apricot. Euryops daisy (*Euryops pectinatus*) is similar, but with bright yellow blooms. Lower-growing plants with a spreading habit include African daisy (*Osteospermum*), gazania (*Gazania*), and the bush monkey flower (*Mimulus aurantiacus*). In mild climates, tender perennials can survive the winter outside, but will only do so in colder areas if potted up and brought into a frost-free greenhouse or conservatory.

Annual climbers

Annual climbers are second to none for speedy summer cover on all sorts of vertical features like screens, walls, obelisks, and other supports. While some nurseries and garden centers sell ready-grown plants in spring, often the only way to enjoy these ultra-quick scramblers is to grow your own.

Sow the seed in pots under cover in early spring, plant out by early summer, and by mid- to late summer plant growth should reach well in excess of 6ft (1.8m) high. Popular varieties to look out for include moonflower (*Ipomoea*), cup-and-saucer vine (*Cobaea scandens*), and purple bell vine (*Rhodochiton atrosanguineum*), while the Chilean glory flower can be treated as an annual in cold areas. Hardy annual climbers include sweet pea, canary creeper (*Tropaeolum peregrinum*), and common nasturtium.

To be sure of success with tender plants, patience is of the utmost importance. Do not put plants outside until all danger of frost has passed, as even a light frost can kill or severely check their growth. Plants that have been raised under cover will need to be acclimatized to the outside environment for a couple of weeks first. This process, called hardening off, involves putting plants out for increasing periods of time during the day and then at night, protecting them if frost is forecast.

Biennials

The life cycle of biennials is longer than that of annuals, but these easy-to-care-for plants are well worth growing for a reliable show of color from spring to early summer. Biennials grow from seed sown during summer, and then theyare

PLANTING -UP A CONTAINER

1 In the base of the pot, put in a 2in (5cm) layer of drainage material like pieces of broken terracotta pot or chunks of polystyrene. Fill the pot about a third full of compost and put the central plants in first.

2 Add a bit more compost and put in the smaller ones around the edge. The final level of the compost should be about 1in (2.5cm) below the rim of the pot to allow room for watering.

GROW AN INSTANT GARDEN IN CONTAINERS

•For virtually instant effect, use plants growing in a variety of containers. Whatever the layout of your garden and however awkward the site may be – and even if there is no garden at all – just plant up and arrange a few pots, and you will have a beautiful overnight display.

•Half-hardy annuals and tender perennials are perfect for pots, because they look spectacular throughout the summer; but many other plants can be grown in containers as well including compact varieties of shrubs, climbers, conifers, perennials, and ornamental grasses.

•Containers can be used all around the garden – in small groups, singly as focal points, and dropped into borders to create a splash of extra color.

3 With all the plants in the pot, fill the gaps with compost and firm gently with your fingers. Water the container thoroughly, using a watering can fitted with a rose.

transplanted in autumn to where they will flower the following year. Most varieties can be raised very easily from seed if you have a spare corner of ground to use as a little nursery plot; if not, there should be a good selection of plants on sale in autumn. Popular spring-flowering biennials include English wallflower (*Cheirianthus cheiri*), woodland forget-me-not (*Myosotis sylvatica*), and English daisy (*Bellis perennis*); they are often planted alongside bulbs to make a riot of color. Summer-flowering varieties include common foxglove (*Digitalis purpurea*) and dame's rocket (*Hesperis matronalis*). Once flowering is over, dig up and compost the plants. However, most biennials will self-seed readily to create a delightful informal look; delay digging them up until the seed pods turn brown, and then scatter the ripe seed.

Bulbs

Bulbs are wonderfully versatile and virtually foolproof, for they already contain their own store of energy. Because of this, most varieties can be grown almost anywhere in the garden. Spring bulbs can be grown under trees and large deciduous shrubs, for the bulbs will be over and done before the permanent plants leaf up and take all the light. Bulbs may be planted in grass, assuming the grass can be left long for a few weeks so the bulbs' leaves can die back. Bulbs can be planted almost anywhere in borders – even under carpets of ground-covering plants – because they will be able to work their shoots through to the light.

There is an enormous range of bulbs on sale, and while it is tempting to try lots of different ones, you will create a much better effect by planting big numbers of just a few varieties. Choose bulbs that flower at different times in order to have a succession of glorious color from late winter right through to early summer. The show starts in late winter with snowdrops (*Galanthus*) and winter aconites (*Eranthis hyemalis*), moves on to the first narcissi (*Narcissus*), then turns into high drama with a wealth of daffodils (*Narcissus*), narcissi, tulips (*Tulipa*), hyacinths (*Hyacinthus*), and many others. As spring moves into summer, the late-flowering varieties of tulips and narcissi fill the gap until the first annuals begin to bloom. Autumn is prime planting time for all spring- and some summer-flowering bulbs. Narcissi and early bulbs like snowdrops and crocus (*Crocus*) must be planted in early autumn, because they need a lot of time to make root growth. Tulips perform best when planted in late fall, because they tend to rot if planted earlier.

While spring bulbs are the most widely planted, many summer beauties are equally good for creating color in a short time. Lilies (*Lilium*) put on a spectacular show, with tall stems topped with huge, exotic-looking blooms in many colors (often with a gorgeous perfume, as well). Lilies perform best when planted in spring and therefore have the shortest time from planting until flowering. Large varieties of ornamental onions (*Allium*) create a dramatic effect with massive, rounded flowers on tall stems, but they must be planted the previous autumn. Finish the gardening year on a high note with massed plantings of crocus, autumn crocus (*Colchicum*), and nerines (*Nerine*), which bloom in mid- to late autumn.

To be sure of success, take care to plant bulbs at the right depth, at the right time, and away from wet soil, which causes rotting. After flowering, foliage must be left to die back naturally so the bulbs can build up energy for next year. Remove the dead flower heads, feed with high-potash fertilizer, and water if the weather is dry. If you cannot stand the sight of yellowing bulb leaves, plant bulbs in mesh containers sold for pond plants, and sink these in the soil so only the handles are showing. Once flowering is over, simply whisk the pot away so the bulbs can die back away from the garden.

Spring displays *Plant bulbs in autumn and reap the rewards next spring. Here, daffodils (*Narcissus*) and tulips (*Tulipa*) combine with red polyanthus (*Primula*).*

Summer bulbs *With bold blooms on tall stems, Allium hollandicum 'Purple Sensation' is guaranteed to grab the limelight.*

PLANT DIRECTORY

HOW TO USE THE DIRECTORY

THE PLANTS IN THE DIRECTORY are listed alphabetically by their botanical or Latin name. When you are looking at each entry, be sure to fold out the extended back flap of the book cover. This will give you an instant guide to the planting symbols shown below each plant's name, which will help you decide where to grow it in your garden. Plant size given is approximately that which is reached after ten years, which gives an indication of where to site each one with a view to its eventual size.

Each entry includes a description of the plant, some hints on where to site it for best effect, its preferred growing conditions and care, and how to prune it. Look for the pruning shears symbol to see how often pruning is required.

The plant hardiness zone rating refers to the average annual minimum temperature—in other words, how cold it gets. However, by taking advantage of sheltered sites and providing winter protection, it is often possible to stretch a plant's range to a zone lower than its rating.

Acer grosseri var. *hersii,* *A. negundo* cultivars

Snake bark maple, box elder

Cultivars of these two species of maple make excellent trees for all but the tiniest gardens. Both grow reasonably fast without becoming too large in the long term and look attractive for a long period of time.

The snake bark maple (*Acer grosseri* var. *hersii*) (zone 6) is noted for its decorative bark, which is boldly green-and-white striped; it also produces large, handsome, lobed leaves that develop beautiful autumn tints.

The box elder (*Acer negundo*) (zone 3) ia a very fast-growing tree, with light green leaves. Cultivars such as 'Elegans' and 'Flamingo' are still fast-growing but are a good deal smaller, and have small lobed leaves that are attractively variegated.

WHERE TO PLANT
Grow in fertile, moisture-retentive but well-drained soil. Site alone in a lawn or border. Both species can be underplanted with a wide variety of low-growing plants, as they do not form a dense canopy of foliage.

CARING FOR PLANTS
Trouble free.

CONTROLLING GROWTH
Remove wayward or crossing shoots in late autumn or winter. Variegated cultivars of box elder can be grown as a bushy shrub by hard pruning every year in late winter. Plants grown in this way look very good if underplanted with a carpet of one variety of ground-cover plants.

Box elder makes a handsome, fast-growing tree. Cultivars with variegated leaves are smaller and suitable for very small gardens.

Akebia quinata

Five-leaf akebia

    12ft (3.6m) as available

Five-leaf akebia (zone 5) has clusters of reddish-brown, cup-shaped flowers, borne in spring, which have a pleasant, spicy perfume. The dark green leaves are divided into five oval leaflets and look good from spring to autumn, and often right through the year if the winter is not too severe. In autumn, if there has been a warm spring and a long, hot summer, this plant bears unusual sausage-shaped, purple fruits. To ensure cross-pollination to obtain fruits, purchase two plants from different sources and grow them close together.

WHERE TO PLANT
Grow in moist but well-drained, fertile soil. In cold areas, plant it against a sheltered wall to protect the flowers from late frosts that can damage the blooms, although the plant itself is hardy. The twining stems will need wires or trellis for support. Five-leaf akebia can also be grown up a pergola, arch, and trellis, or it can be trained up into a tree.

CARING FOR PLANTS
Trouble free.

CONTROLLING GROWTH
No regular pruning is required, but growth can be trimmed as necessary after flowering.

Akebia flowers are strikingly unusual in appearance and have a delicious chocolate-like scent too.

Alchemilla mollis

Lady's mantle

Lady's mantle (zone 3) is an attractive, easy, low-growing perennial that quickly forms large, spreading clumps and readily self-seeds. The lobed, velvety, pale green leaves are especially beautiful after rain or heavy dew, when they hold moisture in tiny "pearls." Lax, loosely-branched stems bear numerous tiny, greenish-yellow flowers, and the stems flop outward to lie over the foliage rather than being held upright.

WHERE TO PLANT
Lady's mantle prefers moist, humus-rich soil, but it is also tolerant of drought. Plant it under trees or large shrubs, or toward the edge of a border where there is room for the flower stems to flop outward.

CARING FOR PLANTS
Trouble free.

CONTROLLING GROWTH
To avoid self-seeding, cut off the faded flower stems before the seeds have a chance to ripen. Cut back to ground level at any time from autumn until spring. After 4 to 5 years, when the plant has formed a large, congested clump, rejuvenate it by lifting, dividing, and replanting it when dormant, discarding the old, woody center.

The flowers of lady's mantle look spectacular in summer, when they form a frothy mass of lime-yellow. Many people avoid this plant because of its habit of self-seeding prolifically, but the problem can be averted by cutting off the faded flowers before the seed ripens.

Amelanchier lamarckii

Apple serviceberry

15ft (4.5m)   12ft (3.6m)

Apple serviceberry (zone 6) is a useful garden tree that establishes itself quickly. This tree looks good from spring to autumn, and it is worthy of any garden; it is particularly useful in a small plot where the number of trees must be limited . Although flowers and fall color are its main attractions, the foliage and fruit are nice, too. In spring, masses of white flowers appear, and at the same time, rounded, bronze-colored young leaves emerge; the leaves later age to dark green. Small purplish-black fruits are borne in late summer, and these are edible when cooked. In autumn, the leaves turn wonderful shades of red and orange before falling.

WHERE TO PLANT
Grow on acid (lime-free), fertile, moist but well-drained soil in sun or partial shade. Neutral soils are tolerated, although the autumn leaf color is less showy in such a site. Plant in a border or as a single specimen.

CARING FOR PLANTS
Trouble free.

CONTROLLING GROWTH
No pruning is necessary, as long as sufficient space for growth has been allowed. If necessary, prune in late winter to early spring by removing entire branches, but take care not to spoil the overall shape.

Gorgeous autumn color is just one of the attributes of apple serviceberry. Offering several seasons of interest, it is ideal for small gardens.

Artemisia 'Powis Castle'

Wormwood

2ft (60cm) 3ft (90cm)

Artemisia 'Powis Castle' (zone 6) is a beautiful foliage plant that rapidly forms graceful, billowing mounds of finely-divided, silvery leaves that are aromatic when crushed. Panicles of silver, yellow-tinged flowerheads are borne in summer, but they are of secondary interest to the foliage. Many people prefer to remove the blooms so that they can enjoy the foliage alone. Whilst many other *Artemisias* are quick-growing, this variety is by far and away the most ornamental of them.

WHERE TO PLANT
Grow in full sun on fertile, well-drained soil. Like many silver-leafed plants, wormwood prefers well-drained soil; it rarely survives on heavy, moisture-retentive ground. In such sites, grow wormwood in a raised bed to ensure good drainage. Site toward the front or at the edge of a border, and use the foliage to enhance and contrast with other brightly-colored flowering plants.

CARING FOR PLANTS
Aphids can be a problem in late summer, but rarely enough to affect the plant's health.

CONTROLLING GROWTH
Prune hard in spring to encourage plenty of fresh, new growth, as unpruned plants tend to become woody and bare at the base.

The delicate silvery foliage of Artemisia *'Powis Castle' can be used to make a handsome contrast to many different border plants.*

Ballota pseudodictamnus

Ballota

18in (45cm) 2ft (60cm)

plant directory

48

Grown for its handsome, gray-green, felted leaves, ballota (zone 8) quickly forms a loose, spreading mound of evergreen foliage. White to pinkish-white, two-lipped flowers are produced, but these are of secondary interest to the foliage. The leaves are aromatic when crushed, although some people find their strong smell unpleasant. The foliage is soft and immensely apealing to touch.

WHERE TO PLANT
Ballota thrives in poor, dry, free-draining soil and full sun. Plant at the edge of a border where it can spread on to paving, but avoid siting it close to a lawn, as the overhanging plant growth will kill the grass beneath. Ballota is also good in raised beds, where it tumbles down slightly and softens the edge.

CARING FOR PLANTS
Do not fertilize or apply organic mulches unless the soil is exceptionally poor.

CONTROLLING GROWTH
Cut back hard in midspring to within 1in (2.5cm) of last year's growth to encourage bushy growth and to avoid woodiness at the base. Overgrown plants are best replaced with fresh plants, as they rarely regrow well if they have been hard pruned.

The soft, felted leaves of ballota are irresistible to touch and stroke, so place this spreading plant near to a path or tumbling over a wall where it can be accessed easily. Woolly foliage is just one mechanism by which plants can conserve moisture, indicating that this is a good choice for dry soils.

Bergenia

Bergenia

Bergenias (zone 4) are clump-forming evergreen perennials that quickly make excellent ground cover in all sorts of garden situations. The glossy leaves are large and rounded—hence the common name "elephant's ears"—and look attractive right through the year. While the foliage of all varieties is dark green from spring to autumn, many varieties change color in winter to rich shades of maroon or red. Large clusters of funnel-shaped, white, purple, or pink flowers are borne on short stems in late winter and early spring, and they show up well against the large leaves.

WHERE TO PLANT
While bergenias prefer humus-rich, moist but well-drained soil, they do tolerate poor soil and will develop brighter winter leaf color under such conditions. They make excellent ground cover at the edges of borders, under trees and large shrubs, and on banks. For the best effect, plant in groups of three, five, or seven of a single variety.

CARING FOR PLANTS
Susceptible to slugs, snails, and caterpillars. Vine weevil may also be a problem in mild areas.

CONTROLLING GROWTH
To keep plants tidy, cut off dead flower stems and remove tattered leaves in late spring. Overgrown, established clumps can be rejuvenated by lifting, dividing, and replanting in autumn.

Colorful bergenia flowers are an immensely welcome sight in the gloomy days of late winter and early spring. The large evergreen leaves provide year-round interest too.

Betula pendula cultivars

European white birch

18ft (6m) 12ft (3.6m)

Quick to establish and grow away, birches (zone 2) are excellent trees for gardens of all sizes. Although decorative white bark is their most notable feature, they also have a graceful shape, yellow-brown catkins in spring, and attractive leaves that turn butter-yellow in fall. Despite their height, birches are suitable for small gardens because they form a lightly-foliaged canopy of branches, enabling a wide variety of smaller plants to be grown beneath.

Several cultivars are well worth selecting: 'Laciniata' has very pendulous branches and finely-cut leaves; 'Tristis' has slender branchlets; and 'Purpurea' has purple-tinged bark and dark purple leaves. There is a weeping cultivar, as well, but it is more space-hungry and less attractive than the upright varieties.

WHERE TO PLANT

Grow in moderately fertile, moist but well-drained soil. Plant in a border, as a single specimen, or in a small group in a woodland garden. Create a multi-stemmed tree by planting three young saplings together in the same planting hole.

CARING FOR PLANTS

Leaves may start to yellow on poor soil, but this can be remedied by feeding. Although there are several pests and diseases that often attack birches, chemical control is rarely necessary. Help plants ward off attack by keeping them in good health with annual mulching and feeding.

CONTROLLING GROWTH

None required.

The white bark of birches looks lovely in winter, and their graceful shape suits all but very small gardens.

Brachyglottis (Dunedin hybrids) 'Sunshine'

Brachyglottis

4ft (1.2m)   5ft (1.5m)

Formerly known as *Senecio*, *Brachyglottis* 'Sunshine' (zone 7) is an easily-grown shrub that grows rapidly and looks attractive throughout the year. The plant forms a wide-spreading mound of rounded leaves that look gray when young due to a covering of white hairs. Large, showy clusters of bright yellow "daisy" flowers are borne over a long period. Despite its height, this is a good plant for ground cover, because it forms a dense mound that suppresses weeds.

WHERE TO PLANT
Grow in well-drained soil and, in cold areas, in a sheltered site. Plant singly or in groups, at the middle to the edge of borders, or massed as ground cover on banks.

CARING FOR PLANTS
Brachyglottis is relatively trouble free. Removing the dead flower heads is not essential, but it will improve the plant's appearance.

CONTROLLING GROWTH
After flowering, cut back any wayward shoots that are spoiling the shape or outgrowing the site. Any frost-damaged shoots should be removed in spring.

The silvery-grey foliage of brachyglottis makes a handsome backdrop to masses of yellow flowers in summer.

plant directory

52

Buddleja alternifolia

Fountain butterfly bush

10ft (3m) 6ft (1.8m)

Fountain butterfly bush (zone 6) quickly forms a large, upright, mound-shaped shrub that will reach the size of a small tree if left unpruned. Over a period of several weeks, slender, arching shoots are wreathed with dense clusters of sweetly-scented lilac flowers which, as the name suggests, are attractive to butterflies. The stems of *Buddleja alternifolia* are clothed with narrow, silvery-green leaves that look attractive from spring to autumn.

WHERE TO PLANT
Grow on fertile, well-drained soil. Plant toward the back of a border or as a single specimen in a lawn.

CARING FOR PLANTS
Give additional support using a short, stout stake, because plants will become top-heavy with age. If desired, the lower shoots can be removed to create a clear stem, and the head can also be trimmed to form a neater standard shape.

CONTROLLING GROWTH
After flowering, cut back flowered shoots to a strong pair of buds. On older plants, completely remove about a quarter of the oldest shoots to encourage new replacement growth.

Aptly named for its graceful weeping branches, the fountain butterfly bush looks glorious in summer when the stems are wreathed with lilac flowers.

Buddleja davidii

Summer lilac

This tall, fast-growing deciduous shrub is invaluable for mid- to late summer color and is beloved by butterflies and moths, which flock to its sweetly scented, nectar-rich blooms. The numerous large flower spikes are made up of hundreds of tiny blooms, each with an orange throat. Many named varieties of Summer lilac (zone 6) are available, and the following selection gives a good sample of the range of colors available: 'Black Knight' (violet-purple), 'Dartmoor' (reddish-purple), 'Empire Blue' (lavender-blue), 'Pink Delight' (clear pink), and 'White Profusion' (white).

WHERE TO PLANT
Summer lilac prefers a well-drained soil that is reasonably low in fertility. Place toward the back of a border or grow as a single specimen in a lawn. For maximum color, underplant summer lilac with spring-flowering, shade-tolerant, herbaceous perennials, as the ground underneath will be left bare for a couple of months after its annual spring pruning.

CARING FOR PLANTS
Summer lilac thrives best on soil that is reasonably low in fertility, so apply annual dressings of fertilizer and nutrient-rich mulches at half-strength.

CONTROLLING GROWTH
Prune summer lilac hard every year in early spring, cutting all stems to within 18in (46cm) from the ground. Neglected, overgrown plants can be severely pruned in early spring and, in most cases, will regrow successfully—even if cut back to a tall stump.

The flowers of summer lilac are irresistible to butterflies. There are many different colors, of which 'Black Knight' is the darkest and most striking.

Campanula poscharskyana

Serbian bellflower

6in (15cm) 3ft (90cm)

Of the many different bellflowers, *Campanula poscharskyana* (zone 4) is the fastest-growing, and it makes excellent ground cover. Clusters of star-shaped flowers, which are lavender-blue with white centers, smother the plant over a very long period and show up well against a mass of toothed, medium green leaves. The variety 'Stella' has bright violet flowers. Campanulas look particularly good when used to underplant roses in a bed or border.

WHERE TO PLANT
Grow in moist but well-drained soil. Serbian bellflower is good at the edges of borders, on a bank, and for covering the ground under trees and shrubs that cast only light shade. With care, it can also establish itself in cracks and crevices between paving slabs and stones. This plant spreads by underground runners and should not be placed near plants of lesser vigor that could be overwhelmed.

CARING FOR PLANTS
Serbian bellflower is susceptible to slugs and snails.

CONTROLLING GROWTH
If the plant is spreading too far, use a spade to chop off the outer sections of the clump.

A rampant grower, Serbian bellflower makes superb ground cover so long as there is no danger of it overwhelming smaller plants nearby.

Campsis

Trumpet creeper

15ft
(4.5m)

as
available

With huge, colorful flowers, bold foliage, and lush, fast growth, trumpet creeper (zone 5) is dramatic and almost tropical in appearance. Clusters of up to 12 trumpet-shaped flowers are borne at the ends of the shoots; the large, pinnate, dark green leaves are coarsely toothed. Yellow trumpet creeper (*C. radicans* 'Flava') is bright yellow; trumpet vine (*C.* x *tagliabuana* 'Madame Galen') is orange-red and is the most free-flowering variety.

WHERE TO PLANT
Grow in moderately fertile, moist but well-drained soil, with a wall, fence, or tree for support. In colder areas, trumpet creeper needs full sun and the protection of a sheltered wall, while in warmer areas it will tolerate a little shade and exposure.

CARING FOR PLANTS
Although trumpet creeper is self-clinging by means of aerial roots, it may take several seasons to secure itself. In the early years, put up a framework of wires on which to train the plant. On young plants, pinch off the growing shoot tips to encourage branching.

CONTROLLING GROWTH
In late winter or early spring, cut back side shoots to within 3 to 4 buds of the main branches, and thin out overcrowded shoots.

Create a tropical feeling with the lush foliage and exotic, brightly colored blooms of the trumpet creeper.

Ceanothus

California lilac

10ft (3m) 6ft (1.8m)

The California lilacs (zone 8) are quick-growing shrubs that look truly spectacular when in bloom, when they are smothered with numerous "powder puff" clusters of flowers that are a beautiful and sometimes intense shade of blue. Flowering time is either spring to early summer or late summer to fall. Popular cultivars include 'Blue Jeans' (medium blue, evergreen, early-flowering); 'Gloire de Versailles' (pale blue, deciduous, late-flowering); and the ground-covering *C. thyrsiflorus* var. *repens* (dark blue, evergreen, early-flowering).

WHERE TO PLANT

Grow in fertile, well-drained soil and in a sheltered site. While not reliably hardy in very cold areas, upright-growing types can be trained against a sunny, sheltered wall, which will often give sufficient protection against severe frosts. Plants grown in this fashion will grow larger and faster than those sited elsewhere. *C. thyrsiflorus* var. *repens* makes good ground cover.

CARING FOR PLANTS

California lilac is susceptible to honey fungus.

CONTROLLING GROWTH

Prune wall-trained plants by cutting back flowered shoots to within 2 to 4 buds of the main branches. Late-flowering varieties should be pruned in spring, while early-flowering ones should be cut back after flowering.

California lilac looks truly magnificent when the whole plant is covered with masses of "powder puff" flowers in gorgeous shades of blue. This variety is C. thyrsiflorus *var.* repens.

Lawson false cypress

Lawson false cypress (zone 5) is a conifer that is narrowly columnar or conical in shape and that has given rise to a huge number of cultivars, many of which are reasonably fast-growing. They make excellent specimen trees, and they are also good for hedging when you require something a little slower than the ultra-fast Leyland cypress (× *Cupressocyparis leylandii*).

Good cultivars include 'Alumii', with blue-gray foliage and a conical habit; 'Columnaris', which is pale blue-gray and columnar in shape; 'Green Hedger', which is bright green and pyramidal; 'Kilmacurragh', which is bright green and narrowly conical; and 'Pembury Blue', which is bright blue-gray and conical in shape.

WHERE TO PLANT
Grow on well-drained soil that is moisture-retentive and neutral to slightly acid. Plant in large borders, in grass, as single specimens, or, in a large area, in groups of three of one variety. For a hedge, plant in a single row spaced 24in (60cm) apart.

CARING FOR PLANTS
Lawson false cypress is susceptible to *Phytophthora* root rot, but it can be avoided by ensuring good drainage.

CONTROLLING GROWTH
Trim hedges any time from late spring to early autumn, but do not cut back into older wood. Avoid trimming specimen plants if at all possible, as pruning spoils the overall attractive shape.

Tall conifers such as Lawson false cypress make excellent specimen trees or hedging plants for year-round foliage. Mature plants are dotted with little cones too.

Choisya ternata

Mexican orange flower

Mexican orange flower (zone 7) offers year-round interest; when grown in its preferred conditions, it quickly forms a dense, upright bush. The stems have palmate dark green leaves that are aromatic when crushed. Many clusters of sweetly-scented pure white flowers are borne in late spring, often with a second flush in late summer or autumn.

WHERE TO PLANT
Grow on fertile, well-drained soil in a sheltered site in full sun. Plant toward the back of a border either alone or in a small group. Whilst hardy enough to thrive in the open border, it dislikes cold winds and is best grown against a wall in cold areas.

CARING FOR PLANTS
Older plants can become very dense and may flop open, causing the stems to split near the base. Heavy snow has a similar effect and should be knocked off as soon as possible.

CONTROLLING GROWTH
Little regular pruning is required, apart from trimming wayward shoots that spoil the shape of the plant. On established plants, remove about a quarter of the oldest shoots in spring to avoid the "flopping" problem.

Smothered in masses of white flowers in summer, Mexican orange flower not only looks spectacular but the blooms have a strong perfume too. The glossy lobed leaves are evergreen as well, making this a plant with all-year appeal.

Chusquea culeou

Bamboo

12ft (3.6m) · 6ft (1.8m)

An extremely handsome, fast-growing evergreen bamboo (zone 7) with smooth, yellow-green or olive-green canes and slender, medium green leaves. As the clump matures and becomes more dense, the branches arch outward to create a graceful shape that is narrow at the base and wider-spreading at the top. When the old leaves fall, the branches and leaf stalks remain to give the plant a "whiskery" look. Papery-white leaf sheaths remain on the young canes for the first year to give a "striped" appearance.

WHERE TO PLANT
Grow in leafy, humus-rich, moist but well-drained soil, sheltered from cold, drying winds. Plant *Chusquea culeou* as a single specimen in a lawn, or in a woodland garden.

CARING FOR PLANTS
New shoots may need protection from slugs in spring.

CONTROLLING GROWTH
If plants are spreading too far, use a spade to chop off the outer sections of rhizome in early spring.

This evergreen bamboo makes a handsome specimen as it matures.

Cistus

Rock rose

This fast-growing, sun-loving shrub is wonderful for summer color in milder areas. Rock rose (zone 7) bears masses of blooms, and while individual blooms only last for a day, they are produced in such profusion as to ensure a long display. The leaves of some species exude a sweet-smelling gum. White rock rose (*Cistus* × *hybridus*) is one of the hardiest of all. It forms a low, wide-spreading plant covered in pointed, very dark green leaves that make a handsome contrast to the pure white flowers; *C.* × *pulverulentus* 'Sunset' forms a low bush that is slightly wider than high, with gray-green leaves and large rose-pink flowers; orchid rock rose (*C.* × *purpureus*), a rounded bush of dark green leaves, bears dark pink flowers that have maroon blotches at the base of the petals. Rock roses are often fairly short-lived, and plants that have become old and leggy are best replaced, because they do not respond well to hard pruning. New plants can be raised easily from cuttings taken in summer.

WHERE TO PLANT
Grow in poor to moderately fertile soil that is very well drained. Rock roses must be grown in full sun.

CARING FOR PLANTS
Trouble free. In cold areas, protect plants with a dry mulch around the base.

CONTROLLING GROWTH
No regular pruning required. Straggly shoots can be trimmed in early spring and dead growth can be removed at the same time. After flowering, pinch back the young shoots to encourage bushy growth.

Rock roses need a sun-baked spot to bear profuse quantities of papery-petalled blooms. 'Sunset' is a popular pink variety.

Clematis, large-flowered hybrids

Clematis

12ft (3.6m) · as available

Grown for their huge flowers—up to 8in (20cm) across—and wealth of jewel-like colors, large-flowered hybrid clematis (zone 5) can achieve a fast rate of growth if they are given optimum growing conditions.

For maximum growth, choose the larger varieties that bloom later in the summer. Good varieties include 'Ernest Markham' (red), 'Gypsy Queen' (violet-purple), 'Henryi' (white), 'Lady Betty Balfour' (violet-blue), 'Marie Boisselot' (white), 'Perle d'Azur' (sky-blue), and 'W.E. Gladstone' (lavender-blue).

WHERE TO PLANT

Grow in deep, fertile, moist but well-drained soil in a sheltered site and with a cool root run. Plant with the top of the rootball about 4in (10cm) below ground level. Train up walls, fences, trellis, free-standing supports, or through an existing, well-established shrub or conifer. Large-flowered hybrid clematis is particularly fussy about growing conditions, so opt for a species clematis if conditions are less than ideal.

CARING FOR PLANTS

Boost flowering with a weekly feeding of high-potash liquid fertilizer in spring and early summer. Clematis wilt is a disease that attacks all or part of the plant, but deep-planted clematis have a good chance of regrowth.

CONTROLLING GROWTH

Cut all stems back to about 18in (46cm) from the ground in late winter.

There are a wealth of flower colors to choose from amongst the large-flowered clematis. Select the most vigorous varieties for the fastest growth, like this beautiful blue-flowered 'Perle d'Azur'.

Clematis montana

Anemone clematis

Most vigorous of the many different clematis, the Anemone clematis (zone 6) makes a breathtaking display of white or pink flowers in spring and early summer. Numerous open blooms with four petals are borne in small clusters all along the branches. The blooms of certain varieties have the added bonus of scent, too, most notably *C.m.* var. *rubens*, *C.m.* 'Elizabeth', and *C.m.* var *wilsonii*. The deciduous foliage is attractively cut-edged and is medium to bronze-green in color.

WHERE TO PLANT
Anemone clematis is an easy plant that will thrive in any reasonably fertile soil. Site where there is plenty of room for it to grow freely, such as on a large wall, a sturdy pergola, or over a well-established tree or hedge. Galvanized wire or mesh is necessary to support the climber on walls and fences.

CARING FOR PLANTS
Plant deeply, with the top of the rootball about 4in (10cm) below ground. This gives the plant a good chance of regrowing if attacked by clematis wilt, a disease that strikes fairly often and which causes part or all of the plant to collapse and die.

CONTROLLING GROWTH
Pruning is only necessary to restrict growth or when the stems have formed a tangled mass. Cut back hard immediately after flowering; pruning later will reduce next year's flowers.

A rampant species that needs plenty of space, the anemone clematis is a superb plant that is smothered in bloom from late spring to early summer. There are white varieties as well as pale pink ones like Clematis montana *var.* rubens.

Clematis viticella cultivars

Italian leather flower

The Viticella hybrids (zone 6) are the most versatile of all the huge genus *Clematis*. Their slender stems grow rapidly through the year to produce sizeable plants by late summer, when they become smothered with masses of small blooms. Flower shape and size vary according to variety, from 2 to 4in (5 to 10cm) across and bell- or star-shaped. Colors include white mixed with green, mauve, or purple; violet-purple; and wine-red. All are single with the exception of the double-flowered 'Purpurea Plena Elegans'.

WHERE TO PLANT

Grow on almost any soil, but away from extremes of wet and dry. Because of their slender, lightweight growth and modest pruning requirements, the Viticellas are ideal for growing through and over other plants for an extra bonanza of bloom. The most vigorous variety, 'Polish Spirit', needs to be partnered with a large, well-established host.

CARING FOR PLANTS

Trouble free.

CONTROLLING GROWTH

In late winter, cut the entire plant back to around 12 to 18in (30 to 46cm) from ground level.

Fast-growing yet well-behaved, Clematis viticella *comes in many different colors.*

Cornus alba cultivars

Siberian dogwood

The Siberian dogwoods (zone 3) are easy to grow, and they quickly form substantial shrubs, offering excellent year-round interest. The most decorative are those with colored or variegated foliage such as 'Aurea', which has leaves of soft gold; 'Elegantissima', which has green and white leaves; and 'Spaethii', which has gold and green foliage. The foliage looks good from spring to autumn; when the leaves fall, they reveal red-barked stems that look attractive all winter.

WHERE TO PLANT
Siberian dogwoods are tolerant of a wide range of soils including wet ground, but avoid very dry soil. Plant in borders, either singly or in small groups. Dogwoods are also good for waterside planting.

CARING FOR PLANTS
After pruning, apply a thick mulch and feed well to encourage new growth.

CONTROLLING GROWTH
Pruning is not essential, but it is recommended to achieve good winter stem color along with a well-shaped plant. Every year in early spring, cut back all shoots to within 6 to 12in (15 to 30cm) of the ground.

Variegated foliage and attractive red stems make Siberian dogwoods ideal for year-round interest.

Cortaderia selloana

Pampas grass

Pampas grass (zone 8) is one of the fastest-growing, most dramatic ornamental grasses. It is spectacular from late summer on, when large plumes of flowers are borne on tall, stout stems. The flowers rise above a tufted clump of slender, arching leaves and last through autumn and often into winter. Once the flowers have become battered by severe weather, they are best removed. 'Sunningdale Silver' is the largest variety, and it has the most spectacular flowers; 'Rendatleri' is slightly smaller, with purplish-pink panicles of flower. 'Aureolinata' has attractive, gold-edged leaves; it is good for year-round interest, but it is slower-growing.

WHERE TO PLANT
Grow in fertile, well-drained soil. Pampas grass looks best when planted toward the back of a border; in this way, other plants can be placed in front to conceal the grassy foliage, which can look dull or tattered for much of the year. Come flowering time, however, the tall plumes can be seen above these other screening plants.

CARING FOR PLANTS
In late winter or early spring, cut off and remove the flower stems, then cut and comb out any dead leaves. Wear stout gloves as protection against sharp leaf edges. Do not set fire to clumps, as is sometimes recommended, as this will kill beneficial insects whilst they are hibernating.

CONTROLLING GROWTH
In spring, large clumps of pampas grass can be lifted, divided, and replanted.

Tall plumes of pampas grass wave gently in the breeze, making a magnificent display from late summer onwards. Site towards the back of a border so that other plants conceal its foliage, which can look untidy for much of the year.

x *Cupressocyparis leylandii*

Leyland cypress

Famed for its rapid growth, Leyland cypress (zone 5) is an immensely popular hedging plant; it quickly forms a tall screen of dark green foliage that is excellent for creating privacy or shelter from wind. Additionally, the dense growth makes a superb nest site for birds.

Varieties with golden foliage like 'Castlewellan' are less vigorous than the species, but they will still easily achieve in excess of 24in (60cm) of growth in a year. While Leyland cypress has received a lot of bad publicity due to its size and speed, it can be kept as a low hedge if pruned regularly right from the start.

WHERE TO PLANT
Grow in any deep, well-drained soil in sun or partial shade. For hedges, space plants 30in (76cm) apart. If a solid hedge is not essential, create an informal screen with plants 10ft (9m) apart in a staggered row. Leyland cypress also makes a good individual specimen tree.

CARING FOR PLANTS
In exposed sites, protect a new hedge with windbreak netting for the first year. Leyland cypress is susceptible to honey fungus.

CONTROLLING GROWTH
Once a hedge has reached the desired height, cut back the leading shoots to 18in (46cm) below the final level, leaving space for growth to bush out. Thereafter, trim in mid-spring and mid-summer. A third cut can be done in late summer or early fall, if necessary. Hedge sides can also be trimmed, but avoid cutting back into old wood, because it will not regrow.

A rampant grower, Leyland cypress makes an excellent fast hedge so long as it is trimmed regularly right from an early stage.

Cytisus

Broom

5ft (1.5m)   4ft (1.2m)

Brooms (zone 6) are speedy, upright to rounded shrubs, which are wonderful for early summer color when they become smothered with sweetly-scented blooms. Numerous hybrids are available with blooms in many colors, usually two-toned or bicolored. Such is the variation in flowers that it is best to buy varieties when they are in flower to be sure of choosing the right ones.

However, brooms are fairly short-lived shrubs, particularly if left unpruned so their growth becomes leggy and bare at the base.

WHERE TO PLANT
Broom thrives on well-drained soil that is low in fertility. Plant it in the middle of a border, alone, or in small groups.

CARING FOR PLANTS
Avoid feeding and transplanting brooms. Plant them out when they are young, and support them with a stake for the first couple of years. If plants become leggy or bare at the base, dig them up and replace them rather than attempting to renovate them through pruning.

CONTROLLING GROWTH
Immediately after flowering, cut back long shoots by half to two-thirds to avoid legginess; do not cut back into old wood.

Speedy but fairly short-lived, broom makes a gorgeous show of scented flowers in early summer and is a very useful plant for poor, well-drained soils. Many colors are available, often with two-toned flowers. This variety is 'Minstead'.

Dicksonia antarctica

Tasmanian tree fern

Spectacular and almost prehistoric in appearance, tree ferns (zone 8) have fibrous brown trunks topped with massive, bright green fronds. While the fronds themselves develop extremely fast, the trunks are very slow-growing; it pays to spend more to buy a decent-sized plant, if your budget permits.

WHERE TO PLANT
Tree ferns must have a shady spot that is sheltered from winds; they are superb as specimen plants, either alone or in a group of three. Plants can be grown in containers in their early years, but later on perform best in the ground. Soil type is largely unimportant, as tree ferns gather water and nutrients using their open rosettes of fronds and their fibrous trunks, rather than using a root system.

CARING FOR PLANTS
Keeping the trunk moist during the growing season is very important. In dry, warm weather, soak it daily by pouring water over the top of the trunk, or crown. Feed once a month during spring and summer by spraying the plant with dilute liquid fertilizer.

During winter, tree ferns are hardy to around 15°F (-9°C), but they need protection during long, cold periods. In very cold areas, grow tree ferns in containers and move them under cover. Otherwise, place a thick layer of straw in the crown, tie the fronds over the top, and wrap the plant in horticultural fleece. Cut off dead or tattered fronds in spring.

CONTROLLING GROWTH
None required.

A spectacular specimen plant for a shady spot, even the smallest tree ferns unfurl huge fronds from the top of a brown, fibrous trunk.

Eccremocarpus scaber

Chilean glory flower

8ft (2.4m)   5ft (1.5m)

This fast-developing climber is excellent for gardeners on a budget—it grows readily from seed and blooms in its first summer. Scrambling up by means of tendrils, Chilean glory flower (zone 8) covers its support with attractive, pinnate, sea-green leaves, and it bears many clusters of tubular, brightly-colored flowers. Available colors include orange-red, carmine red, bright pink, and golden yellow.

WHERE TO PLANT
Grow on fertile, well-drained soil and in a sheltered site. Train up walls or fences, using wire mesh or trellis as a support.

CARING FOR PLANTS
During winter in cold areas, protect the roots with a thick mulch and cover the plant with horticultural fleece. Frost may kill some or all of the shoots but regrowth often occurs from the main stems or from the roots. If regrowth does not occur, however, then new stock can be raised from spring-sown seed.

CONTROLLING GROWTH
Cut back in spring only if necessary to contain growth or to remove frost-damaged shoots.

Easily raised from seed, the Chilean glory flower bears masses of blooms even in its first year.

Elaeagnus x ebbingei

Ebbinge's silverberry

Vigorous and quick-growing, Ebbinge's silverberry (zone 6) forms an upright, slightly arching plant of attractive evergreen foliage. When young, the sea-green, leathery leaves are coated on both sides with silvery scales; the older leaves retain this covering beneath. The creamy-white flowers are very small and are borne close to the leaf axils—often, their presence is only revealed by the discovery of their sweet fragrance. Several variegated cultivars are available, of which 'Limelight' is the fastest-growing.

WHERE TO PLANT
This shrub prefers fertile, well-drained soil, but it will tolerate dry soil and coastal sites. Plant in a border, either alone or in small groups. It also makes a good informal hedge, planted at 30in (76cm) spacings.

CARING FOR PLANTS
If shoots die back, prune the affected growth back to healthy shoots.

CONTROLLING GROWTH
Prune only if necessary in spring, trimming or removing shoots that spoil the shape. Variegated cultivars often "revert" and produce shoots of plain leaves, which should be pruned out as they appear.

Although the blooms of this shrub are tiny they pack a real punch when it comes to scent.

Eriobotrya japonica

Chinese loquat

Chinese loquat (zone 10) is a superb wall shrub for architectural effect; it grows reasonably fast when given favorable conditions, but it creates an impact very quickly due to the sheer size of its leaves. The huge, leathery, dark green leaves are ribbed on the surface and grow up to 12in (30cm) long. Clusters of white, sweetly-scented flowers are produced if the plant is growing in a mild area or after a long, hot summer; flowers are followed by edible, rounded- to pear-shaped, orange-yellow fruits.

WHERE TO PLANT

Grow on fertile, well-drained soil and in a sheltered site, trained on wires or trellis against a sunny wall. In cold areas, grow in a large container and move under cover for the winter.

CARING FOR PLANTS

Plants growing under cover may suffer from mealybugs. In containers, grow Chinese loquat in soil-based potting compost and apply a balanced liquid fertilizer monthly throughout the growing season.

CONTROLLING GROWTH

In spring, prune only if necessary to thin out any overcrowded or crossing stems. Container-grown plants usually need annual pruning to restrict growth.

plant directory

The massive ridged leaves of Chinese loquat create handsome architectural effects in a mild, sheltered site, where fruits may be produced after a hot summer. In cold areas it can be grown in a container and moved under cover for the winter.

Erysimum 'Bowles' Mauve'

Wallflower

30in (75cm)   2ft (60cm)

Erysimum 'Bowles' Mauve' (zone 6) is a vigorous, shrubby perennial that rapidly forms an upright mound of slender, gray-green leaves. Large clusters of mauve flowers are borne over an exceptionally long period. Although there are other hybrids available in alternative colors, none flower for such a long time. Do not confuse the perennial varieties of wallflower with the short-lived perennial English wallflower (*E. cheiri*) that is grown as a biennial. 'Bowles' Mauve' lacks the strong scent that is a popular feature of a number of *Erysimums*.

WHERE TO PLANT
Grow in poor to moderately fertile, well-drained soil that is neutral to alkaline. Plant alone or in a group of three at the front of a border or in a raised bed.

CARING FOR PLANTS
This plant is susceptible to several diseases, including mildew and clubroot, but these can be avoided or mitigated by growing plants in the correct conditions. In cold areas, protect plants with cloches over winter.

CONTROLLING GROWTH
Trim lightly after flowering to prevent plants from becoming leggy.

A delightful cottage garden style plant, this variety of wallflower offers exceptional flowering value with its blooms that can be borne from early summer right into autumn.

Escallonia
'Apple Blossom'

Escallonia

6ft (1.8m) · 5ft (1.5m)

Valued for its attractive flowers and glossy evergreen foliage, escallonia (zone 7) is a handsome, useful shrub that soon forms a substantial, rounded plant. Clusters of nicely-colored flowers—apple-blossom pink, as the name suggests—are borne over a long period and show up particularly well against a background of glossy, dark green leaves. Escallonia grows extremely well in coastal areas.

WHERE TO PLANT
Grow in fertile, well-drained soil in a site sheltered from cold winds. Escallonia is not reliably hardy in cold areas, though plants can be grown against a wall for added frost protection. Otherwise, site in the middle to back of a border, or grow as an informal hedge in mild or coastal areas. Plants for a hedge should be spaced 30 to 36in (76 to 90cm) apart.

CARING FOR PLANTS
Trouble free.

CONTROLLING GROWTH
Trim after flowering, only if necessary.

Ideal for coastal areas and sheltered sites inland, escallonia offers year-round appeal with glossy evergreen foliage and summer flowers.

Eucalyptus gunnii

Cider gum

While many *Eucalyptus* species shoot up extremely fast to form tall, spindly trees, cider gum (zone 7) is unusual in that it can be hard-pruned annually and kept as a handsome foliage shrub. Such pruning ensures that the plant keeps its attractive juvenile foliage, which is rounded and glaucous to medium green in color.

WHERE TO PLANT
Grow in fertile, neutral to slightly acid soil, preferably one that does not dry out, and in a site sheltered from cold winds. Plant as a single specimen at the back of a border or in a lawn.

CARING FOR PLANTS
Cider gums perform best planted when young—not more than one year old—in order to establish a good self-supporting root system.

CONTROLLING GROWTH
Every spring, cut all growth back to within 6in (15cm) of the ground. Plants that have been left unpruned will often survive drastic pruning back to a stump, and can then be pruned annually as described previously.

If left unpruned, cider gum develops into an upright tree, spreading with age, with lance-shaped gray-green leaves. Clusters of cream or white flowers are produced in summer or autumn.

The cider gum can be grown in one of two ways. Hard-pruned annually, it can be kept to shrub size and retains this rounded young foliage. Left untouched, it forms an ultra quick-growing tree with an open, rather spindly shape.

Fallopia baldschuanica

Bukhara fleeceflower

12ft (3.6m)

as available

The fastest of all the fast plants, this rampant climber should only be planted where there is considerable room for it to grow. All too often it is sited in too small a space, and it therefore becomes a nuisance. However, given the right situation, Bukhara fleeceflower (zone 4) has an appealing charm, part of which is the almost tropical luxuriance of its growth. Twining stems are clothed with heart-shaped, medium green leaves, and in late summer the plant looks truly spectacular smothered with large panicles made up of tiny blush-pink flowers.

WHERE TO PLANT

Grow in poor to moderately fertile, well-drained soil, and avoid rich soil where lots of growth will be produced at the expense of flowers. It is best grown where it can clamber over a support, and it is ideal for smothering a shed, garage, or large deciduous tree; it is not good on walls or fences, however, where the sheer quantity of growth quickly becomes untidy. Put up strong galvanized wire for support where necessary, but avoid growing this climber on trellis, which is rarely strong enough in the long term.

CARING FOR PLANTS

Trouble free.

CONTROLLING GROWTH

Prune very hard in early spring and after flowering, as necessary, to restrict growth. Summer pruning reduces the amount of flowers that will be produced.

An exceptionally fast climber, the Bukhara fleeceflower makes a wonderful show of late summer blooms.

Fargesia murieliae

Umbrella bamboo

    8ft (2.4m) 3ft (90cm)

The most adaptable of all the bamboos, the Umbrella bamboo (zone 6) is quick-growing yet, unlike many other varieties, is rarely invasive; it is also tolerant of a wider range of conditions.

The plant forms a tall clump of yellow canes clothed with lance-shaped, bright green leaves; the stems are upright when young and eventually arch gracefully under the weight of foliage. There are several smaller cultivars that are ideal where space is really limited.

WHERE TO PLANT
Grow in fertile soil with plenty of moisture, but avoid waterlogged ground. Unlike many bamboos, umbrella bamboo tolerates sun and wind. Plant as a single specimen, as a hedge or screen, or in a large container.

CARING FOR PLANTS
Slugs may attack young shoots.

CONTROLLING GROWTH
Use a spade to chop off the edges of a clump of plants that needs to be reduced in size. Alternatively, lift and divide large, established clumps, in spring.

Bamboos make attractive specimen plants and this species is quick-growing yet rarely invasive.

plant directory

76

Fatsia japonica

Japanese fatsia

8ft (2.4m) 6ft (1.8m)

A valuable and adaptable architectural plant, the Japanese fatsia (zone 8) forms a large, rounded shrub with huge, deeply-lobed, dark green leaves. The rounded heads of white flowers also have a bold shape. While not outstandingly decorative in their own right, their shape contrasts extremely well with the large leaves; the flowers are also useful in that they appear late in the season when there is comparatively little else in flower. Despite its size, this plant thrives in a big container and hence is useful for planting close to the house.

WHERE TO PLANT
Grow in fertile, moist but well-drained soil; in cold areas, plant in a site that is sheltered from winds. Plant as a specimen in a border, or grow in a large container. This plant is tolerant of coastal sites and atmospheric pollution.

CARING FOR PLANTS
Shoots may blacken and die back in winter if the plant is exposed to cold winds. Cut back damaged growth in spring, if necessary.

CONTROLLING GROWTH
Prune in spring, only if necessary to restrict growth or to remove wayward shoots that are spoiling the plant's shape.

The huge, glossy leaves of the Japanese fatsia create fantastic architectural impact in a shady spot.

Forsythia

10ft (3m) 8ft (2.4m)

Forsythia (zone 5) is an extremely easy and fast-growing shrub; it looks spectacular when smothered in golden yellow flowers, which are borne along the naked branches just before the leaves appear. 'Beatrix Farrand' and *F.* x *intermedia* 'Lynwood' are popular larger varieties with rich yellow flowers that are borne in profusion, while weeping forsythia (*F. suspensa*) is a little less showy. However, flowers are the only attractive feature of this shrub; in small gardens, it is best to opt for one of the more compact varieties, preferably with variegated foliage to give a longer period of interest.

WHERE TO PLANT
Grow in moderately fertile soil that is moist but well-drained (although forsythia tolerates fairly poor soil and dry ground). Plant singly or in a small group, in the middle to back of a border. Weeping forsythia can be trained against a wall.

CARING FOR PLANTS
Forsythia gall may occur, but affected shoots can be pruned out.

CONTROLLING GROWTH
Prune immediately after flowering, cutting back flowered shoots to a strong pair of buds. Once plants are established, cut out about a quarter of the oldest shoots near to ground level to prevent the plant becoming bare at the base. Overgrown shrubs tolerate severe pruning.

The golden flowers of Forsythia x intermedia 'Spring Glory' look superb in spring, but bear in mind that this shrub looks dull for the rest of the year.

Fremontodendron 'California Glory'

California flannelbush

10ft (3m) 10ft (3m)

Free-flowering and spectacular, this vigorous shrub produces masses of blooms over a very long period. The waxy-petalled, saucer-shaped blooms are rich golden yellow and are borne all along the branches. The dark green, lobed leaves look attractive too, and the densely hairy young shoots are covered in scales. Although large and vigorous if left untouched, the California flannelbush (zone 8) can be restricted against a large wall if trained and pruned.

WHERE TO PLANT
Grow on poor to moderately fertile, well-drained soil, preferably one that is neutral to alkaline. In all but mild areas, site in a sheltered spot and train the plant against a wall on wires for added protection against frost. Otherwise, plant toward the back of a border.

CARING FOR PLANTS
In winter, wall-trained plants can be given extra protection with horticultural fleece during periods of severe weather.

CONTROLLING GROWTH
After flowering, prune wall-trained plants by cutting out outward-facing shoots and those that are growing inward. Other side shoots should be cut back to 2 to 4 buds of the main framework. Tie in main branches to the support as they develop. Free-standing plants only need wayward or crossing shoots removed in spring. Wear gloves and clothing to protect the skin, as contact with the foliage and shoots may cause skin irritation.

The waxy-petalled golden flowers of California flannelbush will brighten up a large, sunny wall or the back of a border.

Fuchsia 'Riccartonii'

Fuchsia

Fuchsia 'Riccartonii' (zone 7) is one of the hardiest fuchsias; it is invaluable for color late in the season, as it blooms until halted by frost. Quickly forming an upright mound, the slender stems are covered with numerous small, single, crimson and purple flowers that dangle daintily beneath the branches. Hardy fuchsias such as this variety should not be confused with the numerous cultivars of fuchsia that are frost-tender.

WHERE TO PLANT
Grow in fertile, moisture-retentive but well-drained soil in a site sheltered from strong winds. Site in the middle to back of a border. In mild areas, 'Riccartonii' makes a good informal hedge. In cold areas in spring, plant it in a hollow about 2in (5cm) below ground level, and fill in the hollow with soil during summer to encourage growth below ground.

CARING FOR PLANTS
During winter in cold areas, put a thick, dry mulch around the base of the plant.

CONTROLLING GROWTH
In cold areas the stems tend to die back and will need to be cut back to within 2in (5cm) of the base. In mild areas, prune as required at the same time.

Fuchsia flowers hang underneath the arching stems to make a colorful summer display.

Geranium psilostemon

Armenian cranesbill

The herbaceous geraniums include a huge number of species and cultivars, most of which are reasonably quick-growing and can be planted in groups for immediate effect. However, Armenian cranesbill (zone 6) deserves special mention due to its sheer size and the impact it can create—it rapidly forms a great mound of large, elegant, deeply-cut leaves above which rise masses of brilliant magenta-pink, black-centered flowers. The young leaves are tinted with red in spring and develop wonderful red autumn tints before dying back.

WHERE TO PLANT

Grow on any fertile, deep, moisture-retentive and well-drained soil. Plant in the middle to back of a border, singly or in small clumps.

CARING FOR PLANTS

Although mainly trouble-free, Armenian cranesbill is susceptible to several pests and diseases; however, keeping the plant in good condition will help avoid problems. Usually, canes or grow through stakes are necessary for support; these should be put in place in spring so that plants do not begin to flop, because any bent stems will never completely recover for the rest of the year. Cut back the dead growth any time from winter to early spring.

CONTROLLING GROWTH

In late winter or early spring, plants that have formed large established clumps can be lifted, divided, and replanted.

While nearly all herbaceous geraniums are fast-growing, the Armenian cranesbill packs a real punch due to its sheer size and profusion of flowers.

Gunnera manicata

Giant Rhubarb

Giant rhubarb (zone 7) is a truly eye-catching perennial. Absolutely magnificent for architectural effect, it produces enormous dark-green, lobed leaves that can each be up to 6ft (5.5m) long. Tall, prickly stalks bear individual leaves; massive spikes made up of numerous tiny, greenish-red flowers are followed by rounded, red-green fruit. Both children and adults alike are fascinated by this plant, which can tower over the head of a fully-grown person.

WHERE TO PLANT
Grow on deep, humus-rich soil that is permanently moist, either near water or a marsh. In cold areas, plant out of the wind and in a sheltered site.

CARING FOR PLANTS
In winter, the crown of the plant will benefit from a little protection, so bend the dead leaves over the top. In cold areas, add a thick covering of straw or dry mulch, as well. Protection against slugs and snails may be necessary.

CONTROLLING GROWTH
Giant rhubarb is not invasive, so no controlling measures should be necessary as long as the plant was given sufficient room in the first place.

The leaves of this space-hungry plant grow so large that an adult can often stand underneath. However, it needs a sheltered site or a mild climate.

Gypsophila paniculata 'Bristol Fairy'

Perennial baby's-breath

4ft (1.2m) 4ft (1.2m)

Perennial baby's-breath (zone 6) is a wonderful sight in summer, when the tall, branching stems shoot up and are covered in a froth of starry, pure white flowers, forming a huge mound of blossoms. This plant is mostly valuable only for its flowers, as the narrow, gray-green leaves have no real ornamental value.

WHERE TO PLANT
Grow in deep, light, well-drained soil, preferably one that is alkaline. Site in the middle to back of a border, ideally adjacent to plants like Oriental poppy (*Papaver orientale*) that become dormant by midsummer so the baby's-breath can fill the space that becomes available.

CARING FOR PLANTS
Perennial baby's-breath dislikes root disturbance, so do not move it after planting. Stem rot may be a problem if the soil is not very well drained.

CONTROLLING GROWTH
This plant is not invasive, so simply cut back the dead stems any time from autumn to spring.

Unnoticeable for most of the year, perennial baby's breath erupts into an eyecatching cloud of blossom in summer.

Hebe

Hebe

While hebes (zone 9) come in many shapes and sizes, the larger species and varieties are outstanding for their fast growth and exceptionally long flowering period. Long spikes of colorful flowers are borne through summer and autumn, and even into winter if the season is mild. New Zealand hebe (*H. speciosa*) bears purple-blue flowers, while 'Alicia Amherst' bears rich purple flowers.

WHERE TO PLANT
To produce the most blooms, grow hebes in well-drained soil that is poor to moderately fertile—rich soil encourages foliage at the expense of flowers. In cold areas, choose a site sheltered from cold winds. Grow in the middle of a border.

CARING FOR PLANTS.
During winter in cold areas, tuck a thick layer of straw or dry mulch around the base of the plant to protect it from frost. Hebe's grow quickly and easily from cuttings taken in summer, which is worth doing as insurance against winter damage.

CONTROLLING GROWTH.
Although no regular pruning is required, plants can be cut back in early spring to restrict growth, if necessary.

Hebes are fast and useful plants that come in a range of sizes. 'Youngii' makes excellent ground cover.

Helleborus argutifolius

Corsican hellebore

Corsican hellebore (zone 6) is the fastest-growing of this superb group of garden plants, and it is also the most architectural, creating the greatest impact throughout the year. The dark green leaves alone make a handsome sight, forming a large clump with each leaf divided into three spiny-edged leaflets.

This foliage makes a wonderful background for the large, bold clusters of pale green flowers; the flowers are bowl-shaped and up to 2in (5cm) across, and each one bears prominent stamens. Although reasonably tall, this hellebore also makes good ground cover, forming a spreading mound that is wider than it is high.

WHERE TO PLANT

Grow in moist, fertile soil, preferably one that is neutral to alkaline. Avoid planting in dry or waterlogged ground. This hellebore thrives in dappled shade; it is ideal for planting in borders under trees and large shrubs, where it can be planted alone or in a small group. It is also happy in full sun, particularly in cooler areas. Although hardy, in cold areas it should be planted in a site that is protected from winds.

CARING FOR PLANTS

Snails and aphids may be a problem. Unlike most perennials, this hellebore dislikes being divided and should be left undisturbed if at all possible.

CONTROLLING GROWTH

Remove faded flower stems in summer, as near to the ground as possible. Cut off leaves that become brown or tattered any time during spring to fall.

Both the leaves and flowers of the Corsican hellebore are wonderful for creating architectural impact; the apple-green blooms are borne in spring and early summer.

Hosta sieboldiana 'Elegans'

Hosta

30in (75cm) 4ft (1.2m)

The largest and most spectacular of the huge and diverse cultivars of *Hosta*, the luxuriant foliage of 'Elegans' (zone 5) makes it the obvious choice where size and speed matter. The leaves are heart-shaped, crinkled on the surface, and blue-gray in color; each one can be up to 12in (30cm) wide and long. Upright stems of lilac-white flowers are an added bonus, but foliage is definitely the main attraction. A number of recently introduced large-leaved hybrids are also useful in the fast garden.

WHERE TO PLANT
Hostas need fertile, moisture-retentive, and fairly well-drained soil, but they should never be allowed to dry out. Hostas are ideal for borders, bog gardens, and containers, and ideally, they should be sheltered from wind.

CARING FOR PLANTS
Slugs and snails are a major problem with hostas, and preventative measures must be taken from early spring on, as soon as the shoots begin to emerge. Plants that are growing in containers are easier to protect from these troublesome pests. Cut back dead growth any time from autumn to early spring.

CONTROLLING GROWTH
None required.

While most hostas are rapid growers, this variety is worth singling out for the sheer size of its bold, blue-gray leaves.

Hydrangea paniculata

Panicle hydrangea

Panicle hydrangea (zone 5) is a supremely showy, vigorous, quick-growing shrub that makes a superb display of enormous flowers toward the end of the season. This plant forms an upright shrub of long stems clad with ovate, medium green leaves, each stem ending in a massive flowerhead made up of numerous small blooms. 'Floribunda' has white flowers that develop pink tints with age; 'Kyushu' is creamy white and is the most compact variety; 'Praecox' is similar, but it begins to flower in midsummer, before other varieties; 'Unique' has the largest blooms, which are borne in heads up to 8in (20cm) long.

WHERE TO PLANT
Hydrangeas prefer a lime-free (acid) soil that is moist, well-drained, and rich in humus. Site in a shrub border or as a single specimen in a lawn.

CARING FOR PLANTS
Hydrangeas are prone to a number of pests and diseases, particularly gray mold (*botrytis*), leaf spot, aphids, and red spider mites. Grow hydrangeas in their preferred conditions to mitigate potential problems.

CONTROLLING GROWTH
While regular pruning is not essential, larger flowerheads can be obtained by pruning in early spring—cut back last year's shoots to within several buds of the main framework of branches. Plants treated in this way develop a more upright, pyramidal shape. By contrast, the branches of unpruned shrubs hang over gracefully under the weight of the blooms.

The panicle hydrangea grows quickly and soon produces a marvellous display of late-summer blooms.

Hypericum 'Hidcote'

St.-John's-wort

Easiest and fastest of all the different St.-John's-worts, 'Hidcote' (zone 6) is notable for its long flowering period and its large blooms. The rounded shrub of twiggy branches is clothed with lance-shaped, dark green leaves, and the color of the foliage shows off the golden yellow flowers perfectly. The plant will remain evergreen in mild winters, but it will lose some of its foliage in colder weather. The blooms are cup-shaped and up to 3in (7.5cm) across, and they are borne in clusters of up to six flowers. The first, main flush of bloom is in midsummer, but it continues to produce flowers for many weeks, well into autumn.

WHERE TO PLANT

Grow in moderately-fertile, well-drained soil that is reasonably moist. Plant in the middle to back of a border, singly or in a small group. The greatest amount of flowers are produced in sun, but this plant also grows well in partial shade (although it will bloom a little less freely).

CARING FOR PLANTS

Trouble free.

CONTROLLING GROWTH

No regular pruning is necessary. However, shoots that are spoiling the shape of the plant can be trimmed back in early spring. With older plants, where the bush is becoming congested and overgrown, take out about a quarter of the oldest branches as close to the ground as possible.

Easy and quick to grow, the saucer-shaped golden flowers of Hypericum 'Hidcote' appear right through the summer and into autumn.

Jasminum nudiflorum

Winter jasmine

6ft (1.8m) 8ft (2.4m)

Winter jasmine (zone 6) is a superb, adaptable, and reasonably quick-growing shrub that is invaluable for winter color. From early winter the plant is smothered in clear, bright yellow flowers, which are borne all along the leafless stems. Although a deciduous shrub, the shoots of *Jasminum nudiflorum* are an attractive shade of dark green and make a good contrast to the yelllow flowers.

WHERE TO PLANT
Grow in well-drained soil, preferably one that is fertile (but winter jasmine will tolerate fairly poor soil). This plant can be grown in a variety of ways: against a wall on a support of wires or trellis; closely trained up a post or pillar; or tumbling down a bank or wall.

CARING FOR PLANTS
Trouble free.

CONTROLLING GROWTH
Wall- and pillar-trained plants need to be kept reasonably neat and perform best when pruned annually so that they do not become straggly. Prune immediately after flowering by cutting all the flowered shoots back to within several buds of the main stems.

Cheer up the darkest days of the year with the golden stars of winter jasmine, which thrives almost anywhere.

Jasminum officinale

Jasmine

15ft (4.5m)   as available

This speedy and attractive twining climber has it all: flowers, foliage, fragrance, and adaptability. One of the oldest and most popular garden plants, jasmine (zone 6) bears clusters of white flowers over a long period; the blooms show off beautifully against the dark green leaves, which are divided into small leaflets. The powerful fragrance of the flowers is strongest in the evening. Although jasmine does grow large if unpruned, it can be restricted to at least half its natural size. Several varieties have colored or variegated foliage, and these are less vigorous than the green-leafed forms; they are also less hardy and free-flowering. These include 'Fiona Sunrise', which is suffused with gold, and 'Argenteovariegatum', which has creamy white leaf margins.

WHERE TO PLANT
Grow on fertile, well-drained soil, on a wall, fence, trellis, or pergola. Jasmine needs some form of support, such as wires or trellis.

CARING FOR PLANTS
Trouble free.

CONTROLLING GROWTH
Prune after flowering by thinning out flowered and overcrowded shoots; do not shorten shoots, however, or a mass of thin, spindly stems will result. On established plants, remove a few of the oldest, thickest stems at the same time.

A speedy climber, jasmine can be grown up all sorts of supports, where the handsome dark green foliage makes an attractive backdrop for its pure white, sweetly scented flowers.

Juniperus squamata 'Blue Carpet'

Flaky juniper

Junipers are a large and diverse group of plants with species and cultivars of all sizes and different rates of growth. 'Blue Carpet' (zone 4) is a particularly notable and fast-growing variety, as its prostrate habit makes it a superb plant for ground cover. Spreading, ground-hugging branches are clothed with pointed, intense silvery-blue leaves that look good all year, but which really come into their own for winter color.

WHERE TO PLANT
Grow in any well-drained soil, including chalky, dry, or sandy ground. Junipers prefer full sun but will tolerate light, dappled shade in mild areas. Site toward the edge of a border, in a large raised bed, or on a bank. However, remember that the needle-like foliage is sharp to the touch, so do not plant it where it might brush the legs of passers-by.

CARING FOR PLANTS
Susceptible to aphids and scale insect.

CONTROLLING GROWTH
No regular pruning is required. If pruning is necessary to contain growth, cut back in spring, but take care not to spoil the shape of the plant.

This sun-loving juniper is excellent for ground cover, and its prostrate stems are particularly good for covering banks and slopes. The intense blue foliage looks good year-round.

Kerria japonica 'Pleniflora'

Globeflower kerria

8ft (2.4m)   6ft (1.8m)

Globeflower kerria (zone 4) is a vigorous, easily-grown shrub that quickly forms a tall, dense thicket of upright to slightly arching shoots. It bears masses of bright, golden yellow, pompon-like flowers in mid- to late spring. There are single-flowered forms, but these are less showy in appearance. Despite being deciduous, the bright green color of the shoots gives good winter interest, although there tends to be some winter die-back.

WHERE TO PLANT
This plant is tolerant of most soils and aspects, but it grows best on fertile, well-drained soil. Globeflower kerria can be grown in full shade, although flowers will not be produced as freely. Grow it in a shrub border or in a woodland-style garden.

CARING FOR PLANTS
Trouble free.

CONTROLLING GROWTH
Immediately after flowering, cut back the flowered shoots to young sideshoots on the main stem, or cut close to ground level. On established plants, thin out a few of the oldest shoots. If the plant is spreading more than is desired, dig out some of the outer stems complete with roots.

Studded with golden flowers in spring, globeflower kerria is a quick and tall-growing shrub.

Lavandula angustifolia

English lavender

English lavender (zone 6) is much loved for its aromatic foliage and scented flowers. Despite being a small shrub, English lavender is quick to establish, it flowers freely, and it creates an impact within a short time when planted in groups or as a low, informal hedge. Slender, upright stems bear masses of cylindrical blooms above a rounded bush of long, narrow, gray-green leaves.

All parts of the plant are strongly aromatic when crushed. Varieties include 'Hidcote', which has dark purple flowers and a compact habit, and 'Twickel Purple', which is lighter in color and wider-spreading. The flowers are popular with bees and butterflies.

WHERE TO PLANT
While English lavender tolerates most soils except heavy, boggy ground, it thrives best in well-drained, moderately-fertile soil. Plant in groups at the edges of borders, in raised beds, or as a low hedge with plants in a single row spaced 12 to 18in (30 to 46cm) apart.

CARING FOR PLANTS
Gray mold (*botrytis*) can be a nuisance in damp conditions. Older plants that have not been pruned tend to become woody at the base and "flop" open; these are best replaced with new stock, as lavender rarely regrows successfully if pruned hard.

CONTROLLING GROWTH
In late spring every year, prune the whole plant to the base of last year's growth, but do not cut back into old wood. After flowering, trim off the dead flower stalks to keep the plant tidy.

Beloved for its perfume, English lavender is a fast grower that is perfect for borders and low hedges.

Lavatera

Tree mallow

8ft
(2.4m)

6ft
(1.8m)

This top-performing, fast-growing garden plant not only makes a large, well-established bush in a single growing season, but it also flowers for an incredibly long time. Tree mallow (zone 6) stems bear numerous funnel-shaped flowers, each one about 3in (7.5cm) across, for many weeks, usually right up to the first severe frosts. The lobed leaves are gray-green. The flowers of 'Barnsley' are white with a red eye, and they mature to soft pink; 'Rosea' is dark pink.

WHERE TO PLANT

Grow in light, reasonably fertile, well-drained soil, sheltered from cold winds. Site toward the back of a border, leaving plenty of room to spread. For spring flowers, plant the ground immediately around the base with shade-tolerant ground-cover plants. If space is limited, tree mallow can be trained as a bushy, fan-shaped plant against a wall, fence, or trellis.

CARING FOR PLANTS

Tree mallow is prone to stem rot and rust, although growing it in its preferred conditions will mitigate potential problems. Prune every year, or the plant will become top-heavy, and the stems may split near the base.

CONTROLLING GROWTH

Every year in early spring, cut all stems back to about 6in (15cm) from the ground. To avoid wind damage in winter, shorten all stems by around half in fall.

Create impact within a single season with the ultra-fast growth of the tree mallow. 'Barnsley' is a particularly attractive variety, though any stems that revert and produce plain pink flowers should be cut out immediately.

Leycesteria formosa

Himalayan honeysuckle

Himalayan honeysuckle (zone 7) is a vigorous, graceful, thicket-forming shrub that soon forms a substantial plant; it usually blooms well in its first year. Attractive, tapered, dark green leaves clothe upright, arching stems; the flowers are produced in long, dangling racemes at the ends of the stems. The white flowers are enclosed in dark purple-red bracts, and they are followed by shiny black berries that are popular with birds. Although deciduous, this plant has rich green stems that look very handsome in winter.

WHERE TO PLANT
An easy-going plant, Himalayan honeysuckle thrives in most well-drained soils. Plant in a shrub border or a woodland garden.

CARING FOR PLANTS
In cold areas, choose a site that is sheltered from winds, and thickly mulch the roots in autumn to protect the plant from frost.

CONTROLLING GROWTH
In early spring, to encourage vigorous and bushy growth, cut all stems back to a low permanent framework of branches. Alternatively, the plant can be kept as a larger specimen by cutting back flowered shoots to young sideshoots.

A quick-growing shrub, the Himalayan honeysuckle soon forms a thicket of arching stems. White and claret-colored flowers are borne in summer, followed by berries that are popular with birds.

Ligustrum ovalifolium 'Aureum'

California golden privet

California golden privet (zone 5) is a very fast-growing evergreen shrub, which is particularly notable considering that the majority of evergreens are slow-growing. The gold and green leaves look good all year, but its bright foliage is particularly welcome during winter, both of which make this variety far more garden-worthy than the green-leafed species. The stems are ideal for cutting and are popular with flower arrangers. Unpruned bushes bear creamy white flowers in midsummer (these have a rather unpleasant scent)—that are followed by black berries.

WHERE TO PLANT
California golden privet thrives on any well-drained soil, but it may lose some leaves in winter if sited on poor soils. It is tolerant of sun or shade, although the brightest leaf color comes from plants growing in full sun. For hedging, space plants 18in (46cm) apart. California golden privet responds extremely well to trimming, and it makes an excellent formal hedge or individual shaped topiary. Left untrimmed, it is equally attractive, as it forms a graceful mass of billowing foliage. Site toward the back of a border if plants are to be left untrimmed, while those for formal shaping should be sited according to their planned size.

CARING FOR PLANTS
California golden privet is susceptible to several pests and diseases including aphids, scale insect, and honey fungus.

CONTROLLING GROWTH
In early and late summer, trim hedges and formal specimens twice a year. Rejuvenate mature specimens that are becoming bare at the base by pruning out several of the largest branches as close to the ground as possible.

Attractive golden foliage makes California golden privet an excellent choice for fast hedges.

Lonicera nitida 'Baggesen's Gold'

Boxleaf honeysuckle

5ft (1.5m) — 3ft (90cm)

Attractive year-round golden foliage and reasonably quick growth make this easily-grown shrub a valuable addition to the garden. Tiny oval leaves, which are bright yellow in spring and darken as the summer progresses to become bronze-colored in winter, stud arching stems. Boxleaf honeysuckle (zone 4) forms an upright dome shape.

WHERE TO PLANT
Grow on any reasonable, well-drained soil. The yellow coloring is most pronounced in sun; the more shade there is, the greener the foliage becomes, and it is a very attractive light green color. Grow in a shrub border or as a hedge with plants spaced 18 to 24in (46 to 60cm) apart.

CARING FOR PLANTS
Trouble free.

CONTROLLING GROWTH
Pruning is not essential, but a light trim in spring will encourage a greater proportion of brightly-colored foliage. Hedges can be trimmed in spring and again in late summer.

Boxleaf honeysuckle is a handsome evergreen for low hedges or border planting.

Lonicera periclymenum

European honeysuckle

Beloved not only for its strong scent, but also for its colorful flowers, European honeysuckle (zone 4) is an easily-grown, popular climber that establishes itself and grows quickly. Clusters of creamy white, trumpet-shaped flowers age to yellow inside; the outside color varies according to the variety. The flowering times vary too: 'Belgica' has deep pink flowers, and it blooms early in the season for several weeks; 'Graham Thomas' is the most vigorous, bearing pure cream to yellow flowers through summer and often into autumn; 'Serotina' has rich purple-crimson flowers throughout summer. The plant's scent is most pronounced in the evening, and it often attracts moths.

WHERE TO PLANT

Grow in fertile, humus-rich, moist but well-drained soil, preferably in part shade (but plants will tolerate full sun if there is plenty of moisture at the roots). The twining stems will grow on a range of supports, including an arch, a pergola, on trellis, or into an established tree. Site where the evening fragrance of the blooms can be appreciated to the full.

CARING FOR PLANTS

European honeysuckle is prone to aphids, particularly if grown in full sun. Powdery mildew may also be a problem in summer if the plant is short of moisture during dry spells.

CONTROLLING GROWTH

Immediately after flowering, cut back the stems to healthy young growth. Mulch annually to keep up the moisture-retaining quality of the soil.

A fast-growing twiner, European honeysuckle makes a lovely show of perfumed flowers. This variety is Lonicera periclymenum 'Belgica'.

Macleaya cordata

Plume poppy

8ft (2.4m) 3ft (90cm)

Plume poppy (zone 4) is a truly outstanding perennial that is invaluable for creating height in a short space of time, and it looks good from spring to autumn. Large, lobed, gray- to olive-green leaves, which are white beneath, clothe tall stems all along their length. In mid- to late summer, the tops of the plume poppy's stems develop huge panicles of tiny, buff white or flesh-colored flowers.

Although the plume poppy is tall, it rarely needs staking. This species is often confused with the similar *M. microcarpa*, which can be much more invasive.

WHERE TO PLANT
Grow in any reasonable well-drained soil, preferably one that is moderately fertile, and in a site that is sheltered from cold winds. However, plume poppy will tolerate most soils and part shade. Site in the middle or toward the back of a border, with low plants in front. This plant is beautiful from top to bottom, and, therefore, it is immensely useful for filling a narrow border alongside a wall or fence, and it can even be used as a summer-only screen.

CARING FOR PLANTS
Slugs may attack young shoots. Cut back the dead stems in late winter to early spring.

CONTROLLING GROWTH
Usually, none is required. If the clump is spreading too far, either chop off the outer portions with a spade, or lift, divide, and replant a large established clump.

A marvellous perennial for architectural impact in a short space of time, the plume poppy is attractive in both flower and foliage. Even better, its tall stems rarely need staking.

Malus

Crab apple

15ft (4.5m)   12ft (3.6m)

Crab apples (zone 5) make exceptionally good garden trees, because they offer at least two seasons of interest: spring flowers are followed by decorative fruits in autumn, and the fruits of some varieties can persist well into winter. A few varieties have the added bonus of attractively colored foliage.

M. × *adstringens* 'Hopa' is wide-spreading with dark pink, white-centered flowers and bright red fruit; *M.* × *moerlandsii* 'Profusion' is a spreading tree with bronze-green leaves, purple-pink flowers, and reddish-purple fruit; *M.* × *schiedeckeri* 'Red Jade' has a weeping habit and bears white- to pink-flushed flowers and bright red fruit; *M.* × *zumi* var. *calocarpa* 'Golden Hornet' forms a rounded head of branches and bears white flowers; these are followed by golden yellow fruit that lasts for a particularly long time; 'Royalty' has purple leaves that turn wine-red in autumn, along with crimson flowers and dark red fruit.

WHERE TO PLANT
Grow in fertile, moist but well-drained soil, preferably in full sun (partial shade is tolerated). Site alone, in a border, or on a lawn.

CARING FOR PLANTS
Crab apples are susceptible to a number of pests and diseases including aphids, apple scab, canker, and mildew. However, keeping plants in good health by thorough ground preparation, feeding, and mulching will help keep trees problem-free.

CONTROLLING GROWTH
No regular pruning is required.

The decorative fruits of crab apples often last well into winter. Those of 'Golden Hornet' are particularly long-lasting.

Meconopsis cambrica

Welsh poppy

An enthusiastic self-seeder, the Welsh poppy (zone 6) is an easy plant, and it is excellent for rapidly colonizing the ground under trees and shrubs. The plant forms a low clump of ferny, fresh green foliage; slender stems each bear a single shallow, cup-shaped flower. Two colors are available: clear lemon-yellow and pale orange. While the bulk of the blooms are produced in late spring to early summer, this plant will continue to flower into fall if deadheaded regularly.

WHERE TO PLANT
Welsh poppy thrives on almost any soil, except for very dry ground. Plant in a border, under trees, or in a woodland garden.

CARING FOR PLANTS
Trouble free.

CONTROLLING GROWTH
To avoid self-seeding, cut off the dead flower heads before the seeds ripen. Alternatively, hoe off the young seedlings in late summer. Mature plants develop deep roots, so it is advisable to remove unwanted plants whilst they are still small and easy to kill off.

Welsh poppy is a charming ground-cover plant that quickly colonizes bare soil, even under trees and large shrubs. The blooms are produced over a long period too.

Melianthus major

Honey flower

8ft (2.4m)   5ft (1.5m)

Despite its tender nature, honey flower (zone 9) is well worth growing—even in cold areas as a seasonal plant—because of its rapid growth and gorgeous foliage. The stout, hollow stems are clothed with large, blue-gray to gray-green leaves; each leaf is divided into a dozen or so curved leaflets that have attractive, deeply serrated edges. The foliage is the main attraction, but the crimson-brown to deep red flowers are handsome, as well. For more flowers, grow this plant on poor soil.

WHERE TO PLANT
Grow outdoors in mild areas in moist but well-drained, moderately fertile soil, in a sheltered site. In cold areas, grow the plant in a large container in loam-based potting compost, and move it into a greenhouse for the winter.

CARING FOR PLANTS
Honey flower is generally free of pests and diseases. To give extra winter protection outdoors, mulch the soil thickly to protect the roots. Where temperatures fall only to around 25°F (-4°C) plants often die back, but they will sprout again in spring.

CONTROLLING GROWTH
If necessary, shorten any lanky shoots that spoil the plant's shape. However, vigorous plants that need to be restricted can be cut back hard in spring.

Despite being tender in many locations, honey flower is well worth growing for its huge and handsome leaves.

Miscanthus sinensis

Japanese silvergrass

8ft (2.4m)

24in (60cm)

Japanese silvergrass (zone 4) is a tall, graceful, ornamental grass; it quickly forms good-sized clumps that create height and useful vertical interest in a border. The slender, upright stems form narrow clumps and look somewhat like bamboo. From late summer and into autumn, large panicles of silky "flowers" or spikelets are borne on tall stems above the foliage. A number of varieties are available in different sizes. Some are grown more for their decorative foliage than for their flowers, such as 'Morning Light', 'Variegatus', and 'Zebrinus', which have leaves that are edged, striped, or banded with white. Free-flowering varieties include 'Rotsilber', 'Malepartus', and 'Silberfeder'.

WHERE TO PLANT
Japanese silvergrass prefers moderately fertile, moist but well-drained soil, but it tolerates most soils (except for ground that is very wet in winter). Plant it in a border or as a free-standing specimen. This plant also associates well with water.

CARING FOR PLANTS
Trouble free.

CONTROLLING GROWTH
Cut back all growth in winter or early spring. Established clumps can be divided in early spring.

An attractive ornamental grass, some varieties of Miscanthus—like 'Morning Light'—produce particularly good displays of flowers.

Nepeta x faassenii

Blue catmint

18in
(45cm)

24in
(60cm)

Blue catmint (zone 4) is an excellent, easy ground-cover plant and is popular for its fast growth, aromatic foliage, and soft coloring. Long, lax stems clothed with small, silvery-gray leaves spill out to form a spreading clump. Numerous sprays of pale lavender-blue flowers appear in abundance in midsummer and in smaller quantities until well into autumn. As the name suggests, cats adore this plant and love to nibble and roll in its foliage—so much so that the clump can become flattened unless a few stems of a prickly plant are tucked into the center as a deterrent. The flowers are also popular with bees.

WHERE TO PLANT
Grow in any well-drained soil, preferably in sun (but it will tolerate partial shade). Site near the edge of a border with space for the plant to grow outward, or so it can spread onto a path or paving to soften the hard edges and release its scent when brushed against. Blue catmint is also good in a raised bed, where it will tumble over the edge.

CARING FOR PLANTS
Blue catmint can become straggly later in summer; to keep plants neat and to encourage a second large flush of flowers, cut them back by half after the first main flowering. Cut back dead growth in early spring.

CONTROLLING GROWTH
None is required.

Beloved by cats and popular with bees, blue catmint makes colorful ground cover in a sunny spot. Plant where its aromatic foliage can be fully appreciated.

Papaver orientale

Oriental poppy

Rapidly forming large clumps, Oriental poppies (zone 4) produce huge flowers that make a fairly short but spectacular display—their vivid blooms grow up to 8in (20cm) across.

Many colors are available, including crimson-scarlet, maroon-red, white, grayish-pink, and salmon-pink; the large silky petals are often boldly marked with black or dark-crimson blotches at the base. The large seed capsules have some decorative value. The long flower stems tend to sprawl and flop outward, and the plant dies back by midsummer.

WHERE TO PLANT
Grow in deep, fertile, well-drained soil. Site toward the edge of a border alongside plants that flower in late summer—in this way, they will take over the space that will be left bare.

CARING FOR PLANTS
To prevent the flowers from flopping over, put a grow-through plant support in place in early spring, as soon as growth begins.

CONTROLLING GROWTH
It is rarely necessary to control growth, but established plants can be lifted, divided, and replanted in autumn. However, try to avoid moving Oriental poppies from their original site, as pieces of root left behind tend to regrow.

Oriental poppies make an eyecatching display of enormous flowers in summer, but need to be partnered with plants for later in the season as the foliage dies back by midsummer.

Parthenocissus henryana

Silver-vein creeper

While all *Parthenocissus* species are vigorous climbers that create a wonderful cover of greenery, the foliage of silver-vein creeper (zone 8) looks attractive for the longest period of time. The palmate, 3 to 5-lobed leaves are a soft shade of dark green, and the veins are conspicuously silver. In autumn the foliage makes a spectacular display, when all the leaves turn fiery red. This plant self-clings by way of disc-like suckers on the tips of the tendrils. However, young plants can take a little time to become entirely self-clinging and benefit from training onto canes or wires for the first year or two.

WHERE TO PLANT
Grow in any reasonably fertile, well-drained soil, and in a sheltered site in cold areas. Although this species tolerates sun or shade, the most conspicuous veining is achieved in partial shade. Plant on a large wall, on a fence, or plant to grow into an established tree.

CARING FOR PLANTS
Trouble free.

CONTROLLING GROWTH
In early winter, prune as necessary to restrict growth (prune again in summer if necessary). Keep growth trimmed away from gutters, drainpipes, and window frames.

The handsomely-marked leaves make the silver-vein creeper the most attractive species of Parthenocissus *to grow. Self-clinging once established, the stems of mature plants need to be kept trimmed away from woodwork and drainpipes.*

Passiflora caerulea

Bluecrown passionflower

This vigorous climber speedily clambers over supports and looks good for much of the year; it has showy flowers and attractive foliage, as well as colorful fruits after a favorable summer. The curiously-shaped flowers are a mixture of purplish-blue and ivory-white; the name of passionflower comes from the suggestion that the parts of the flower represent the instruments of Christ's passion. Bluecrown passionflower (zone 8) is covered with dark green leaves that are divided into 3 to 5 leaflets; they will remain evergreen as long as the winter is not severe. After a hot summer, bright orange, egg-shaped fruits will be produced; the pulp surrounding the seeds is edible.

WHERE TO PLANT
Grow on any moderately fertile, well-drained soil. Bluecrown passionflower must have a sunny, sheltered site, except in mild areas, where it will tolerate partial shade. Plant against a wall, fence, trellis screen, or pergola. This plant climbs using tendrils, so some form of support will be necessary.

CARING FOR PLANTS
In cold areas, train closely against a sunny wall for maximum frost protection. Mulch the roots with a thick, 3in (8cm), layer of chipped bark to provide extra insulation against frost.

CONTROLLING GROWTH
In early spring, prune as necessary to restrict growth. Frost-damaged shoots and any shoots that have died back in the cold can be cut back at the same time.

A very fast-growing climber, the bluecrown passionflower bears striking and unusually-shaped blooms that show off well against glossy, lobed leaves.

Paulownia tomentosa

Princess tree

If unpruned, princess tree (zone 5) will gradually form a large tree that bears lilac flowers in late spring. However, you can grow a summer jungle plant by hard pruning the princess tree annually; it will then produce several stems that can be thinned to a single fast-growing, giant shoot that will eventually bear enormous leaves. Each light-green, shallowly-lobed leaf will grow to around 3 feet (90cm) across.

WHERE TO PLANT
Grow in fertile, well-drained soil, sheltered from wind in cold areas. Plant as a young sapling or raise from autumn- or spring-sown seed. Plant toward the back of a border or as a specimen plant.

CARING FOR PLANTS
Plant in spring to allow the plant plenty of time to establish before winter. In cold areas, young plants benefit from some winter protection in their first year.

CONTROLLING GROWTH
Every year in early spring, cut the entire plant back to 2 to 3 buds from the base. After pruning, mulch with well-rotted compost or manure, feed, and keep well watered to encourage lots of new growth.

Create an exotic jungle effect by annual hard-pruning of the princess tree so that it produces a single stem clothed with enormous leaves.

Penstemon

Beardtongue

Beardtongues (zone 7) form a large group of evergreen perennials that are wonderful not only for their summer color, but also because they quickly form low bushes of glossy foliage topped with stems of flowers. Beardtongues are exceptionally free-flowering, and they produce many slender stems covered with numerous tubular-shaped blooms.

They come in a range of lovely colors, including many shades of pink, white, and mauve; often they have contrasting white throats. there is an exceptionally wide range of colours available, so it is best to choose plants when in flower to be sure of finding the right colours.

WHERE TO PLANT
Grow in fertile, well-drained soil, preferably in full sun (but they will tolerate a little shade). Plant at the middle to edge of a border, preferably in small groups for greater impact.

CARING FOR PLANTS
Remove dead flower stems to prolong flowering. Tall varieties will benefit from staking or supporting with a grow-through support early in the year, to avoid wind damage. In cold areas, protect the roots with a thick covering of straw or bracken as protection from frost in winter.

CONTROLLING GROWTH
Shorten stems by around half to two-thirds in early spring, but only if necessary to restrict growth or to remove frost-damaged shoots. Tall varieties benefit from this treatment annually, or the stems can flop over and break at the base.

The beardtongues are superb border plants that flower over a long period. Many varieties are available; this one is 'Blackbird'.

Perovskia atriplicifolia

Russian sage

Russian sage (zone 6) grows quickly and makes a superb display late in the season. The tall, graceful stems are topped with open spires of lavender-blue flowers that last for many weeks; they are borne in such profusion that they appear as a haze of blue. The gray-white stems and toothed, silver-gray leaves look very attractive, as well, and the foliage is sharply aromatic when crushed.

WHERE TO PLANT
Grow in poor to moderately fertile, very well-drained soil. Russian sage is tolerant of chalky soil and coastal sites. This is a good plant for the middle of a border, where the tall stems create some rapid height, and their attractive shape contrasts well with many other plants.

CARING FOR PLANTS
Trouble free.

CONTROLLING GROWTH
Although pruning is not strictly necessary, Russian sage grows best if cut back to within 6in (15cm) of the ground in spring to encourage bushy, free-flowering growth.

An ardent sun-lover, Russian sage quickly produces tall stems of lavender-blue flowers.

Ideal for covering the ground, Himalayan fleeceflower makes an attractive display of summer flowers. This variety is 'Superba'.

Persicaria affinis cultivars

Himalayan fleeceflower

Himalayan fleeceflower (zone 3) is a handsome, useful, carpet-forming plant; it makes good ground cover in a short space of time, blooms over a long period, and looks good for much of the year. The lance-shaped, medium green leaves form a dense mat that gives rise to long spikes of brightly-colored flowers. In autumn, the leaves turn bronze-red or rich brown, providing good winter color. The dead flowers can be left on the plant, where they turn an attractive shade of brown, providing further winter interest.

The best and most vigorous variety is 'Superba'—also known as 'Dimity'—with blush-pink flowers that mature to crimson. Smaller and less vigorous are 'Darjeeling Red' and 'Donald Lowndes', both of which have flowers that open pale pink and mature to dark pink or red.

WHERE TO PLANT
Grow in any moisture-retentive soil. For ground cover, plant in groups at the front of a border, under a tree that does not cast a dense shade, or on a bank. Himalayan fleeceflower is also useful for planting in drifts in a woodland garden. This is a vigorous plant, and it should be given plenty of room to spread.

CARING FOR PLANTS
Trouble free.

CONTROLLING GROWTH
None is usually required. In spring or fall, established plants can be divided. Trim off the dead flowers in winter when they become untidy, or before growth starts in spring.

Phalaris arundinacea 'Picta'

Ribbon grass

This is an attractive ornamental grass that is very easy and quick to grow; however, ribbon grass (zone 4) should be planted with care, as it becomes very invasive. Flat, slender, upright stems are boldly striped with white, and the pale green flowers—which are produced on tall stems—are particularly graceful.

WHERE TO PLANT

Grow in any soil including wet ground and pond margins, but avoid soil that is very dry. This grass makes excellent ground cover in places where it won't encroach upon other plants; avoid planting it in a mixed border, however, unless the roots are restricted (see 'Controlling Growth' below).

CARING FOR PLANTS

To encourage brightly variegated foliage throughout the year, cut back all but the new shoots in early summer.

CONTROLLING GROWTH

If grown as a marginal plant at the edge of a pond, place it in a submerged container. The same treatment is also suitable for border plants to prevent them from becoming invasive. Grow ribbon grass in a large, sunken pot or bucket that has had the bottom removed.

Although handsome of leaf, beware the invasive tendencies of ribbon grass and contain the roots to prevent it taking over your border.

Philadelphus

Mock orange

Renowned for the gorgeous scent of its bowl-shaped white blooms that smother the branches in summer, mock orange (zone 5) is a quick-growing shrub that comes in a range of cultivars of varying sizes.

Smallest of all is 'Manteau d'Hermine', which has double flowers and grows to just 3ft (90cm) high. 'Belle Etoile' and 'Sybille' grow to 4 to 5ft (3.5 to 4.5m) and both have single flowers. Largest of all is 'Virginal', which grows to at least 8ft (7m) and has double blooms. The flowers are the only real feature of this shrub, because the oval, medium green leaves have no great appeal. Partner with a late-flowering clematis for extra blooms if desired.

WHERE TO PLANT

Grow in any reasonably fertile, well-drained soil. Plant in the middle to back of a border, or the larger varieties can be planted in a woodland garden. Take care to buy a variety of a size that suits the available space; if the plants are pruned hard to restrict their overall growth, they will rarely bloom well.

CARING FOR PLANTS

Powdery mildew and aphids may be a problem.

CONTROLLING GROWTH

Immediately after flowering, cut back flowered shoots to a strong pair of buds or to new shoots lower down. On older plants, remove about a quarter of the oldest shoots as close to ground level as possible to encourage new growth from the base.

A quick-growing shrub, mock orange is a fragrant delight in early summer. However, it offers little interest at other times of year.

Phygelius

Cape fuchsia

Cape fuchsia (zone 8) is a small, exotic-looking shrub that establishes rapidly and throws up many tall flower stems in its first year. Each stem is clothed with numerous showy, colorful blooms, which are tubular with lobed mouths.

There are three main species, *Phygelius aequalis*, *P. capensis*, and *P. × rectus*, of which many cultivars offer a wide range of colors. These include creamy yellow, orange-red, pale red, deep pink, and orange, often with lobes and throats in contrasting colors.

WHERE TO PLANT
Grow in fertile, moist, but well-drained soil. In cold areas, grow cape fuchsia against a sunny, sheltered wall. In milder areas, it tolerates partial shade; it can also be grown out in the middle of a border. Wall-trained plants tend to grow taller than average, while those in borders are best treated as herbaceous perennials and should be cut down every spring.

CARING FOR PLANTS
In frost-prone areas, cape fuchsias can be protected with a thick mulch of straw around the roots. During the summer, remove dead flower stems to encourage further flowering.

CONTROLLING GROWTH
In early spring, hard prune leggy shoots on wall-trained plants. Border plants should be cut back to within 3 to 6in (7.5 to 15cm) of the ground.

Quick to grow either in the border or against a wall, cape fuchsia makes a wonderful long-lasting display of exotic-looking blooms. This variety is 'African Queen'.

Phyllostachys aurea, P. nigra

Golden bamboo, black bamboo

These handsome bamboos (zone 6) make quick-growing, graceful specimens—their long, slender, medium to dark green leaves and colored canes add to their appeal and extend their season of interest to year-round. The glossy canes are brown-yellow and lustrous black, respectively, although the plants need to be 2 to 3 years old for canes to develop their full color. Both species form dense clumps—the golden bamboo is stiffly upright while the black bamboo has an arching habit.

WHERE TO PLANT

Plant in rich, moisture-retentive soil, sheltered from winds in cold areas. *P. aurea* will tolerate soil that is fairly dry. Grow at the back of a border, as a specimen, in a woodland garden, or as a screen. These bamboos also make excellent container plants and should be grown in a large pot in loam-based potting compost.

CARING FOR PLANTS

Slugs may damage new shoots.

CONTROLLING GROWTH

Pruning is rarely necessary in cool to temperate climates. Overgrown or spreading clumps can be lifted and divided in early spring.

Glossy dark stems of black bamboo look attractive year-round although the plant is particularly handsome when in leaf. For an alternative color, opt for the golden bamboo with yellow-brown canes. Both species make eyecatching specimens for the border or a large container.

Physocarpus opulifolius

Common ninebark

Common ninebark (zone 5) soon forms a rounded bush of arching branches and handsome foliage, making it a useful contribution to a border from spring to autumn. The 3-lobed leaves vary in color: those of 'Dart's Gold' are bright yellow when young and age to yellow-green in summer. 'Dart's Gold' is much more garden-worthy than the similar 'Luteus', which loses its gold coloring earlier. By contrast, 'Diablo' is a striking shade of purple; clusters of white, pink-tinged flowers are followed by red berries, but foliage is the main attraction.

WHERE TO PLANT
Grow in fertile, moist but well-drained soil, preferably one that is acid. Site in the middle to back of a border.

CARING FOR PLANTS
Trouble free.

CONTROLLING GROWTH
Annual pruning is not essential, but it will help the plant achieve better foliage color. After flowering, cut back branches to strong young growth. On established plants, remove about a quarter of the oldest branches close to ground level.

The large-lobed leaves of common ninebark come in gold or purple and supply tremendously useful color from spring to autumn.

Potentilla fruticosa 'Katherine Dykes'

Bush cinquefoil

This extremely easy, long-flowering shrub soon forms a loose mound of twiggy stems, which are clothed with tiny leaves and studded with numerous brightly-colored flowers. While all the many different cultivars of bush cinquefoil are quick-growing, 'Katherine Dykes' (zone 4) is the most vigorous, tallest variety. Masses of saucer-shaped flowers, which are a rich shade of canary yellow, are borne over a long period. Other varieties offer an exceptionally wide range of colors, including white, pink, orange-red, pale yellow, and cream. However, the twiggy stems of cinquefoils do not look attractive in winter, so avoid planting in a prominent position.

WHERE TO PLANT

Grow in poor to moderately fertile, well-drained soil. Plant in the middle to back of a border, alone or in a small group. Bush cinquefoils make good plants for informal, low hedges; they should be planted 30in (76cm) apart. While cinquefoils prefer full sun, a little light shade is tolerated; however, be sure that the shade is not from an overhanging tree that will take moisture from the soil.

CARING FOR PLANTS

Trouble free.

CONTROLLING GROWTH

Pruning is only necessary to restrict growth; the flowered shoots can be cut back to within 1 to 2in (2.5 to 5cm) of last year's growth, and several of the oldest branches can be removed close to the ground, to avoid the bush becoming dense and bare in the center.

Of the many different and quick-growing bush cinquefoils, 'Katherine Dykes' is the most vigorous. Masses of yellow flowers are borne right through summer.

Prunus avium 'Plena'

Double mazzard cherry

Quick to establish itself, the double-flowered form of the mazzard cherry (zone 3) is a wonderful sight in spring, when it is smothered in clusters of pure white flowers; but it has additional ornamental attributes that make it worthy of inclusion in most gardens.

The tree develops a pleasing shape, forming an upright to spreading, rounded head of branches clothed with large, ovate, dark green leaves, which are bronze when young. In autumn, the foliage develops showy, bright red tints before falling; and in winter, the red-banded bark looks attractive, as well.

WHERE TO PLANT
Grow on any reasonably fertile, moist but well-drained soil. Plant as a single specimen in a border and underplant with shade-tolerant, low-growing plants; plant in grass; or plant in a woodland garden. In a large garden, this tree looks good when planted as a group of three.

CARING FOR PLANTS
Several pests or diseases may cause holes in the leaves, but chemical control is rarely necessary. Keep the tree in good health by annual mulching and feeding to encourage plenty of healthy new growth.

CONTROLLING GROWTH
None required.

Blossom is synonymous with spring and the double mazzard cherry puts on a wonderful display. Attractive fall color and decorative bark add to the appeal of this quick-growing tree.

Prunus laurocerasus cultivars

Common cherry laurel

This tall, fast-growing evergreen is grown primarily for its large leaves. Common cherry laurel (zone 6) is very useful for screening, particularly in gloomy sites, because the leaves are glossy and reflect light. However, neglected plants quickly become very large, particularly in mild climates where there is a lot of rain; therefore, the most vigorous cultivars should be avoided in such sites. Unpruned plants produce upright racemes of white flowers (the smell of these is unpleasant to some people). These are followed by dark red to black cherry-like fruits that are toxic if eaten.

Vigorous varieties include 'Rotundifolia', which has plain green leaves, and 'Etna', which is similar but with orange-red young shoots. The most compact variety is 'Castlewellan', with green leaves that are boldly marbled and speckled with creamy white.

WHERE TO PLANT
Grow on any reasonably fertile, moist but well-drained soil (although laurel will tolerate most soils except for shallow chalky and boggy ground). Plant to create a screen as necessary, either singly, in a small group, or as a hedge with plants spaced 24 to 30in (60 to 76cm) apart.

CARING FOR PLANTS
Several pests and diseases may attack laurel, but chemical control is rarely necessary.

CONTROLLING GROWTH
In early to mid-spring, and again in midsummer if necessary, prune to remove straggly shoots and restrict growth. On older plants, remove several of the oldest shoots near the base to encourage new growth. Overgrown plants tolerate hard renovation pruning.

A fast evergreen which is invaluable for screening and hedging, common cherry laurel has glossy green leaves, and white flowers in summer if left unpruned.

Ribes sanguineum 'Pulborough Scarlet'

Winter currant

This is an easy, reliable, and vigorous shrub that soon attains a good size and makes a superb show of bloom early in the season. The branches bear small, dark-red, white-centered flowers in long, dangling racemes, which grow up to 4in (10cm) in length and are produced in great numbers. The lobed, toothed, dark green leaves are not very attractive, so bear in mind that flowers are the only real attraction of this shrub. However, its vigor and open branching habit make 'Pulborough Scarlet' (zone 6) a good informal hedge.

There are more compact varieties, but these are also less vigorous, including 'King Edward VII', which has dark red flowers, and 'Tydeman's White', which has pure white flowers. The golden-leaved form 'Brocklebankii' should be grown in light shade to avoid leaf scorch.

WHERE TO PLANT

Grow in any reasonable, moderately fertile, well-drained soil. Plant toward the back of a border, or grow as an informal hedge with plants spaced 30in (76cm) apart.

CARING FOR PLANTS

Aphids and powdery mildew may be a problem.

CONTROLLING GROWTH

Immediately after flowering, cut back all flowered shoots to young lower growth or to a strong pair of buds. On established plants, remove about a quarter of the oldest stems, cutting them back close to ground level. Hedges should be trimmed back at the same time.

Winter currant makes a bold splash of color in spring with masses of red flowers. Ideal for the back of the border, it also makes a good informal hedge.

Rosa rugosa

Rugosa rose

While most shrub roses establish themselves quickly and make decent-sized plants, this species is particularly worthy of note because of its vigorous growth, long season of interest, and tolerance of poor growing conditions. Large, single, cupped flowers grow up to 3in (7.5cm) across and have bold clusters of golden stamens that contrast well with the silky petals. Rugosa rose (zone 2) blooms over a long period of time, and the purple-pink flowers show up well against the bold, dark green foliage; in fall, flowers are followed by large, rounded, orange to orange-red hips that last well into winter. The stems are extremely prickly. *R. rugosa* 'Alba' has pure white flowers and hips that are larger than those of the species.

WHERE TO PLANT
Although this rose thrives in fertile, moisture-retentive, well-drained soil, it is tolerant of poor conditions and even sandy soil. Grow in the middle to back of a border, or as an informal and intruder-proof hedge with plants spaced 30in (76cm) apart.

CARING FOR PLANTS
Trouble free.

CONTROLLING GROWTH
In late winter after their first year, plants perform best when pruned to half to two-thirds of their height every year. Harder pruning will give fewer but better-quality flowers on a compact bush. On older plants, remove one or two of the oldest stems, cutting close to ground level. If you need to restrict growth, then shorten stems by up to a third and reduce side shoots by half.

Tough and easy to grow, the rugosa rose makes a good show of summer flowers which are followed by large, bright red hips that persist into winter.

Rosa Gamebird series

Ground-cover rose

Roses with a spreading habit are immensely useful for clothing large areas of ground, and the Gamebird varieties (zone 4) are by far the most vigorous and quick-growing. Their long, prickly stems rapidly spread to form a prostrate carpet of foliage that is studded with flowers through the summer. 'Grouse' has single dainty, pale pink, fragrant blooms; 'Partridge' has single pure white flowers that are strongly scented; and 'Pheasant' bears cupped, double, clear pink blooms. All varieties have glossy, medium green leaves, and all are disease-resistant.

WHERE TO PLANT
Gamebird roses grow best on fertile, moist but well-drained soil, but they are reasonably tolerant of poor conditions. Site where there is plenty of room for plants to spread, preferably in small groups of a single variety for best effect. These roses look particularly good when trailing down a bank or tumbling over a wall.

CARING FOR PLANTS
Trouble free.

CONTROLLING GROWTH
In late winter to early spring, cut back as necessary to restrict growth. A hedge trimmer can be used to prune the bulk of the growth on large, established plants; then use shears to remove about a quarter of the oldest stems close to the ground.

One of a small group of ultra-vigorous roses, 'Pheasant' is ideal if there is a lot of ground to cover.

Rubus thibetanus

Tibetan bramble

This fast-growing, suckering shrub has something to offer right through the year: Tibetan bramble (zone 6) is valued not only for its attractive foliage and handsome winter stems, but also for its flowers and berries.

The divided, dark green leaves are heavily coated with white hairs, giving the foliage a silvery appearance. In winter, however, Tibetan bramble really comes into its own; the arching, prickly shoots are coated with a white "bloom," creating an eye-catching display through the gloomiest months of the year. Small red-purple flowers are followed by rounded black fruit, although the leaves and stems are the main attraction. This species is often sold under the name 'Silver Fern'.

WHERE TO PLANT
Grow in well-drained, moderately fertile soil. Site in a large border or a woodland garden (in groups of three or more plants for the best effect) and against a dark background so the stems show up well in winter.

CARING FOR PLANTS
Trouble free. Feed and mulch immediately after pruning to encourage strong new growth.

CONTROLLING GROWTH
In early spring, cut back all stems to within 6in (15cm) of the ground, removing any dead stems at ground level.

In winter, the white stems of the Tibetan bramble stand out beautifully against a dark background. From spring to autumn the silvery leaves look attractive too.

Salix

Willow

The shrubby willows (zone 2–6) make superb, exceptionally quick-growing garden plants, and they offer splendid ornamental value at different times of the year. Depending on the variety, their attributes include spring catkins, decorative foliage, and colorful winter stems. *Salix alba* var. *vitellina* 'Britzensis' forms a rounded shrub and is grown for its colorful winter bark—its stems are a vivid shade of orange-red; elaeagnus willow (*S. elaeagnos*) is a wide bush clothed with narrow, gray-green leaves; rosegold pussy willow (*S. gracilistyla* 'Melanostachys') forms a low, open shrub that looks particularly good in early spring, when it is covered with showy black catkins that have red anthers; sandbar willow

(*S. irrorata*) is a large, upright bush with purplish stems that have a white "bloom" and attractive silvery-pink catkins. Although many gardeners avoid willows because of the exceptionally vigorous nature of certain species, the ones listed here make good garden plants.

WHERE TO PLANT
Although willows thrive on damp ground, they do well on any reasonable soil that is not too dry. Grow in the middle to back of a border, singly or in a small group.

CARING FOR PLANTS
Willow anthracnose may be a problem.

CONTROLLING GROWTH
S. alba var. *vitellina* 'Britzensis' should be hard pruned every second year, pruning all stems to 6in (15cm) in late winter. Others can be pruned as necessary at the same time.

The colorful stems of Salix alba *var.* vitellina *'Britzensis' bring welcome color to the garden in winter.*

Salvia officinalis 'Purpurea'

Purple sage

Purple sage (zone 6) is a small but immensely useful shrubby plant that rapidly forms a low mound of long, puckered leaves. Its value lies in the coloring of its foliage, which is rich purple when young and matures to grayish-purple. This subtle shade and its rounded shape make it an extremely good contrast to many border plants.

In summer, purple sage bears well-branched stems of violet-purple flowers for many weeks. The leaves are aromatic when crushed and can be used in cooking. Other varieties of sage with colored foliage are available, but none are as reliable or as quick-growing.

WHERE TO PLANT
Grow in well-drained soil that is reasonably fertile and moisture-retentive. Site at the edge of a border, preferably in small groups for the best effect.

CARING FOR PLANTS
Trouble free.

CONTROLLING GROWTH
No regular pruning is required, but plants that have become leggy can be pruned by half in mid-spring. Older plants that have become tall and very bare at the base are best replaced with fresh stock.

Small yet quick-growing, purple sage is a tremendously useful border plant as its purple foliage makes an attractive contrast to many other plants. The leaves can be used for culinary purposes.

Sambucus

Elderberry

8ft
(2.4m)

6ft
(1.8m)

The ornamental cultivars of elderberry (zone 4) are quick, easy, and tremendously useful garden plants. They are valued primarily for their decorative pinnate (leaflets that are arranged featherwise along the stem) foliage, which is golden or purple. Some varieties have the added bonus of showy summer flowers.

European red elder (*Sambucus racemosa* 'Plumosa Aurea') has finely cut leaflets that are bronze-yellow when young, but which age to gold. The foliage of *S. nigra* 'Guincho Purple' is dark green at first, but then it turns blackish-purple and makes a superb contrast to the large clusters of white, pink-tinged flowers. In autumn, the leaves turn red before falling. These decorative varieties should not be confused with European black elder (*S. nigra*), which self-seeds freely and can become a nuisance.

WHERE TO PLANT
Grow on any reasonably fertile, moist but well-drained soil. Plant at the back of a border. The foliage of the golden elderberry tends to scorch in full sun; in warm areas, it is best to plant it in light shade, where the coloring will become softer but will remain attractive.

CARING FOR PLANTS
Black fly may be a problem on young shoots. After pruning, feed and mulch the plant well to encourage vigorous new growth.

CONTROLLING GROWTH
In early spring, cut back all stems to within 2 to 3 buds of the base to encourage plenty of large, brightly-colored young leaves.

The leaves of the elderberry look good from spring to autumn, opening bronze-yellow and ageing to gold.

Santolina

Lavender cotton

Lavender cotton (zone 7) is a small shrub that is immensely useful for its attractive year-round foliage and colorful display of summer flowers; it quickly attains a rounded shape that becomes lax with age. The finely divided foliage is bright green, gray-green, or silver, depending on the species, and it is aromatic when crushed. In summer, button-like flowers top numerous slender stems; the flowers vary in color from pale yellow to bright yellow, according to the variety.

WHERE TO PLANT
Grow in well-drained soil that is poor to moderately fertile. Site at the edge of a border or a raised bed, singly or in small groups. Lavender cotton also makes a good, low, informal hedge, with plants spaced 12 to 18in (30 to 46cm) apart.

CARING FOR PLANTS
Trouble free. Do not mulch or feed plants unless the soil is very poor.

CONTROLLING GROWTH
In spring, cut back flowered shoots to within 1in (2.5cm) of last year's growth. After the shrub flowers, trim off the dead flower heads.

The button-like yellow flowers of Santolina chamaecyparissus *contrast well with its gray foliage.*

Solanum crispum 'Glasnevin'

Chilean potato tree

A beautiful, long-flowering climber for mild areas, the Chilean potato tree (zone 8) rapidly spreads to cover large areas of wall. The flowers are admired for their color—the deep violet-purple flowers with their central sheaves of orange stamens make a good color contrast. The blooms are borne over a long period, right through summer and into autumn, and sometimes even winter in very mild areas. The ends of the stems bear large clusters of flowers; yellowish-white fruits that are toxic if eaten follow the flowers.

WHERE TO PLANT
Grow in moderately fertile, moist but well-drained soil that is neutral to alkaline. Plant against a sheltered, sunny wall in cold areas. Wires or trellis are needed for support.

CARING FOR PLANTS
The Chilean potato tree is susceptible to aphids and red spider mites. Tie in young shoots regularly to prevent growth from becoming tangled.

CONTROLLING GROWTH
Immediately after flowering, cut back side shoots to within 3 to 4 buds of the main stems. Thin out overcrowded shoots at the same time.

Quick to cover walls, fences, or trellis, the flowers of the Chilean potato tree contain a handsome color combination—violet-purple flowers with a central sheaf of orange stamens. Even better, the flowers are produced over a very long period and often last into winter in mild areas.

Spartium junceum

Spanish broom

    8ft (2.4m) 8ft (2.4m)

A vigorous and very quick-growing shrub, Spanish broom (zone 6) is a tall plant that is covered over a long period with large, showy, golden yellow, pea-like flowers. The slender shoots are clothed with small, narrow leaves; the stems remain green after the foliage has fallen, so the plant stays fresh-looking throughout winter.

WHERE TO PLANT

Grow in moderately fertile, well-drained soil. Site at the back of a border or against a sheltered wall in cold areas. This plant grows particularly well in coastal areas.

CARING FOR PLANTS

Trouble free.

CONTROLLING GROWTH

In early spring, trim back any straggly or wayward shoots. At the same time, rejuvenate older plants that have become leggy by hard pruning them almost to ground level.

The golden flowers of Spanish broom open from early summer and are often produced into early autumn.

Spiraea nipponica 'Snowmound'

Nippon spiraea

   4ft (1.2m) 5ft (1.5m)

Although most spiraeas are easy and fast-growing plants, Nippon spirea (zone 5) is the fastest, most garden-worthy cultivar of all. Forming a rounded shrub with graceful, arching branches clothed with small, rounded, dark green leaves, this plant is a wonderful sight in midsummer when the long branches are smothered in clusters of pure white flowers. Avoid other cultivars of *S. nipponica,* as this one is by far the best.

WHERE TO PLANT
Nippon spirea prefers fertile, moist but well-drained soil (although it will tolerate most conditions, except for dry ground). Plant in the middle to back of a border, singly or in a small group, or in a woodland garden.

CARING FOR PLANTS
Trouble free.

CONTROLLING GROWTH
Prune immediately after flowering, cutting back flowered shoots either to strong lower growth or to a pair of buds. On established plants, remove a couple of the oldest branches close to ground level.

'Snowmound' lives up to its name when the whole of this compact shrub is smothered in pure white flowers.

Stipa gigantea

Giant needle grass

Giant needle grass (zone 8) is a fast-growing, large ornamental grass and is supremely versatile despite its size. A low clump of arching, narrow green leaves bears a spectacular sheaf of huge oat-like flowers that are borne in large panicles on tall, slender stems. The flowers open purple and quickly ripen to a rich harvest yellow.

Despite their size, these flowers are open and airy, and, rather than creating a visual barrier, they can be looked through; therefore, this is a wonderful plant for creating height almost anywhere in the garden. The tall stems generally withstand wind well. The flowers create a touch of drama not only by their sheer size, but also by moving about in the slightest breeze, bringing life and movement to the garden.

WHERE TO PLANT
Grow in light, well-drained, moderately fertile soil. Site anywhere in a border, as the airy stems do not obstruct the view, even if they are planted right at the front of the border.

CARING FOR PLANTS
Trouble free. Dead flower stems can be cut back at any time during winter to early spring. At the same time, remove any dead leaves to keep the plant looking tidy.

CONTROLLING GROWTH
None is required. Large, established plants can be divided from mid-spring to early summer.

Most graceful of all the ornamental grasses, the giant needle grass looks glorious when in flower from summer into autumn and is a superb plant for creating height within a border.

Symphoricarpos × *doorenbosii cultivars*

Snowberry

5ft (1.5m)   5ft (1.5m)

Grown for its attractive autumn fruits that last well into winter, snowberry (zone 4) is a tough, easily-grown shrub that quickly forms a small thicket of arching to upright shoots. Small clusters of bell-shaped, greenish-white flowers emerge in summer, and they are popular with bees; however, berries are this plant's main feature. 'Mother of Pearl' has arching branches and bears white berries that are nicely flushed with pink; 'Magic Berry' has rose-pink berries and is upright in habit.

WHERE TO PLANT
Snowberry grows well in any reasonably fertile, well-drained soil and is tolerant of poor soil. Site in a border, a woodland garden, or grow as a low hedge with plants spaced 24in (60cm) apart. Grow in sun to produce the best crops of berries.

CARING FOR PLANTS
Trouble free.

CONTROLLING GROWTH
No regular pruning is required, but straggly shoots can be trimmed in early spring. Overgrown plants can have some of their branches removed at ground level at the same time.

Bring color to the autumn garden with varieties of snowberry such as 'Magic Berry'.

Tamarix tetrandra

Salt cedar

This graceful, easy, fast shrub soon develops into a large bush of thin, wiry growth; it will reach small-tree size if not cut back. However, unpruned salt cedars become rather leggy and unbalanced with weak flowering stems, so annual pruning is recommended.

In early summer (or sometimes in late spring in mild areas) the Salt cedar (zone 6) becomes a cloud of soft pink bloom—multitudes of tiny flowers in plume-like clusters emerge all along the arching stems. At first, the emerging leaves are barely visible, but later they become an attraction in their own right, with tiny needle-like or scale-like leaves creating a feathery effect.

WHERE TO PLANT
Grow in light, well-drained soil that is poor to moderately fertile. Salt cedar thrives in coastal sites, where it stands up well to strong winds and can be planted as a screen or a windbreak. Away from the sea, plant it in a sheltered site toward the back of a border.

CARING FOR PLANTS
Trouble free. Immediately after planting, cut back plants almost to ground level to encourage strong, branching growth.

CONTROLLING GROWTH
As soon as flowering has finished, cut back the flowered shoots to a strong pair of buds or lower basal growth. On established plants, remove about a quarter of the oldest stems.

A graceful shrub or small tree, the salt cedar has attractive foliage and is spectacular when covered in plumes of pink flowers. This easily-grown plant does particularly well in a coastal location and is also happy in sheltered spots inland.

Thuja plicata 'Atrovirens'

Western red cedar

15ft (4.5m) 4ft (1.2m)

A handsome conifer that is immensely useful for hedging, the Western red cedar (zone 3) can attain around 18 to 24in (46 to 60cm) of growth in a year, and it is a very useful and more handsome alternative to the faster-growing Leyland cypress (x *Cupressocyparis leylandii*). The scale-like foliage is medium to dark green, and it is wonderfully aromatic when crushed. This plant responds well to trimming and makes an excellent formal hedge; it is a faster-growing alternative to yew (*Taxus baccata*), which is a popular but fairly slow-growing hedging conifer.

WHERE TO PLANT
Grow in deep, fertile, moist but well-drained soil (although dry conditions will be tolerated) in a site sheltered from strong winds. Plant in a single row spaced 24in (60cm) apart.

CARING FOR PLANTS
Susceptible to aphids and scale insects.

CONTROLLING GROWTH
Trim in mid- to late spring and again in late summer.

For a reasonably quick formal hedge that stands up well to trimming, the Western red cedar is second to none. The foliage is delightfully aromatic when crushed too.

Verbascum

Mullein

6ft
(1.8m)

24in
(60cm)

These short-lived perennials or biennials are second to none for creating spectacular vertical interest in borders, their tall flower spikes shooting up, seemingly out of nowhere, in summer. Mulleins' (zone 6) tall stems, which are single or sometimes branched, are covered in numerous small, saucer-shaped, brightly-colored flowers that open over a long period, so that those on the lower part of the stem have finished blooming before the top ones have opened. The stems rise from a basal rosette of large, softly-textured leaves that look attractive in their own right, even if they are not as eye-catching.

One of the largest species is silver mullein (*Verbascum bombyciferum*), which bears bright sulfur-yellow flowers; 'Gainsborough' is soft yellow; and 'Pink Domino' is deep rose pink. There are a number of smaller species and cultivars that are as quick to grow but which lack the size to create the same impact.

WHERE TO PLANT
Grow in well-drained soil that is low in fertility, preferably one that is alkaline. On fertile soils the growth becomes more lush and plants need staking. Site in the middle to back of a border or in a gravel garden. Grow in a sheltered site to avoid wind damaging the tall stems.

CARING FOR PLANTS
Powdery mildew may be a problem. Cut back the dead flower stems in winter.

CONTROLLING GROWTH
None is required.

Unnoticeable for much of the year, mullein shoots into the limelight in summer when its tall, brightly colored flower spikes appear.

Verbena bonariensis

Brazilian verbena

5ft
(1.5m)

24in
(60cm)

Brazilian verbena (zone 7) is a tall, graceful perennial that grows extremely fast and produces slender, airy stems topped with clusters of lilac-purple flowers; it also self-seeds readily. The flowers are displayed over a very long period, often lasting into winter if the weather is favorable. The foliage is mostly gathered in a low basal clump, with just a few of the lance-shaped, wrinkled, dark green leaves clothing the lower parts of the flower stems.

The tall, airy stems of Brazilian verbena are marvellous for creating rapid height anywhere in a border. This plant self-seeds readily too.

WHERE TO PLANT
Grow in any moderately fertile, well-drained soil, preferably one that is reasonably moisture-retentive (but dry ground is tolerated). Grow in groups or drifts anywhere in an informal border. Because this plant propagates itself readily, it is possible to have a large group of plants from just a single specimen within a year or two.

CARING FOR PLANTS
Powdery mildew can be a problem, especially on dry soils. Although not reliably hardy in cold areas, a thick winter mulch of straw will often provide sufficient protection. Delay cutting back dead stems until spring to provide extra frost protection.

CONTROLLING GROWTH
This plant self-seeds freely, which creates an attractive informal effect but may be a nuisance. To avoid self-seeding, remove the faded flower heads before the seeds ripen.

Veronica peduncularis 'Georgia Blue'

Speedwell

While many Veronica species make reasonably fast plants for borders, speedwell (zone 6) is outstanding for ground cover because of its length of flowering and compact but rapid growth. Of the several cultivars available, 'Georgia Blue' (also known as 'Oxford Blue') is by far the most free-flowering, producing upright clusters of tiny, deep blue flowers with a contrasting white eye. While spring to summer is the main flowering period, it is not unusual for flowers to begin to appear in late winter. The blooms contrast well with the tiny leaves, which are medium green in summer and dark green tinged with bronze in winter.

WHERE TO PLANT
Grow in moderately fertile, moist but well-drained soil. Plant at the edge of a border or on banks, preferably in small groups for the best effect.

CARING FOR PLANTS
Downy mildew and powdery mildew may be a problem.

CONTROLLING GROWTH
None required. In summer, plants can be trimmed after flowering if necessary.

A small but superb ground-cover plant, 'Georgia Blue' is particularly useful as the shoots root as they spread, allowing pieces of the plant to be detached and planted elsewhere. Flowers appear sporadically throughout the year, with the main flush produced in spring and early summer.

Viburnum rhytidophyllum

Leatherleaf viburnum

8ft (2.4m) 6ft (1.8m)

Grown for its magnificent evergreen foliage, leatherleaf viburnum (zone 6) is a quick, tough, extremely tolerant plant that will thrive almost anywhere. The huge, dark green leaves are very deeply veined and are glossy on the surface, making a handsome contrast not only to the clusters of creamy white flowers, but also to the glossy red berries that emerge later on. The flowers are rather insiginificant compared to the handsome foliage.

WHERE TO PLANT

Leatherleaf viburnum thrives in any reasonably fertile soil, but it will grow in all but the most extreme conditions. It is excellent not only for screening, either singly or in small groups, but also as a structure plant for the back of a border, where its dark foliage makes a good contrast to plants that have pale flowers and foliage. In cold areas, plant in a site sheltered from cold winds as this plant needs a little protection to develop its foliage to its best.

CARING FOR PLANTS

Susceptible to honey fungus.

CONTROLLING GROWTH

None is required. However, any pruning that is necessary to restrict growth can be done in late winter to early spring.

The leatherleaf viburnum comes into its own during winter with its ridged, evergreen leaves and spent flowerheads. Tall and fast-growing, it is ideal for screening and for the back of a border.

Viburnum tinus

Laurustinus viburnum

    6ft (1.8m) 4ft (1.2m)

Laurustinus viburnum (zone 7) is an easily-grown, reasonably fast evergreen that is excellent for winter interest and year-round structure. Although the glossy dark green leaves look handsome all year, the flowers are the main attraction—they are produced in abundance from mid- to late winter, and often well into spring, as well.

The flat heads of bloom are made up of numerous tiny white flowers, which are followed later on by black berries. Before the flowers open, the reddish buds look attractive for many weeks.

WHERE TO PLANT

Grow in any reasonably fertile soil that is moist but well-drained. Plant toward the back of a border, in small groups for screening, or as an informal hedge. Although laurustinus viburnum grows happily in shade, it will flower more freely when given a reasonable amount of sun.

CARING FOR PLANTS

Susceptible to whitefly, viburnum beetle, and honey fungus.

CONTROLLING GROWTH

Prune only if necessary to restrict growth by cutting back shoots immediately after flowering has finished.

Flowering from mid-winter onwards, the white or pink-flushed flowers of the laurustinus viburnum are invaluable for color at this time of year.

Vinca major 'Variegata'

Large variegated periwinkle

This attractive ground-cover plant needs to be sited with care because of its extreme vigor, but it can be extremely useful in the right situation. Large, rounded, medium green leaves that are boldly edged with white clothe arching shoots; the foliage provides a handsome contrast for the blue-violet flowers, which grow up to 2in (5cm) across and are produced over a long period. However, large variegated periwinkle (zone 7) spreads rapidly, because the shoots root where they touch the ground, creating many new plants. Avoid planting the green-leafed species, which is exceptionally invasive but with none of the appeal of the variegated variety.

WHERE TO PLANT
Grow on any reasonable soil, except for very dry ground. Plants flower best when given a reasonable amount of sun; however, periwinkle will also thrive in shade, where the brightly variegated foliage can be very cheerful. Plant in groups as ground cover on banks, under trees and shrubs, or in a woodland garden.

CARING FOR PLANTS
Susceptible to rust.

CONTROLLING GROWTH
Do not plant where it is necessary to restrict growth, or digging up the young, new plants will become a regular job. Keep growth tidy by cutting the whole plant back in late winter using shears. A large patch of periwinkle can be trimmed with a power trimmer.

A rampant yet useful ground-cover plant, the large variegated periwinkle has white-and-green leaves all year which provide a handsome contrast to the blue spring flowers.

Weigela

Weigela

Easy and quick to grow, weigela (zone 4) forms a rounded bush and makes an attractive show of brightly colored flowers in late spring and early summer. The showy blooms are funnel-shaped; they are borne all along the arching branches, either singly or in small clusters.

Many varieties have plain green leaves and no great attraction apart from their flowers, so for maximum interest, choose varieties that have variegated or colored foliage. These include *Weigela florida* 'Foliis Purpureis', with soft purple-green leaves that tone beautifully with the pale pink flowers. *W. f.* 'Variegata' has the same flowers with green-and-white foliage, although the combination doesn't work quite as well in this case. *W.* 'Briant Rubidor' has yellow to yellow-green leaves and ruby red flowers.

WHERE TO PLANT
Grow in any fertile soil that is reasonably well drained. Site in the middle to back of a border, in a group of three if the border is a large one. *W.* 'Briant Rubidor' performs best in partial shade, because the golden foliage can scorch in full sun.

CARING FOR PLANTS
Susceptible to honey fungus.

CONTROLLING GROWTH
Immediately after flowering, cut back flowered shoots to strong buds or young lower growth. On established plants, remove around a quarter of the oldest shoots close to the ground.

An easy and useful border shrub, weigela comes in many varieties. The variegated ones offer the best and longest-lasting interest.

Index

index

Acknowledgments

The publishers would like to thank the following gardens and nurseries for allowing us to photograph their plants and gardens: David Ward at The Beth Chatto Gardens; Matthew Wilson at Hyde Hall, Essex; Forest Lodge Garden Centre, Farnham; The Greenhouse, Kingsbury, London; and The RHS Garden, Wisley, Surrey.

Collins & Brown 24, 25, 37, /Gardening Basics 16, 23, 35, 46, 51, 52, 56, 58-59, 89, 98, 121, /Plants for Free 44, 44-45, 105, 112, /Plants for Small Spaces 28, Weekend Gardener 22, 26, 27, 29, 34; **John Glover/Garden Picture Library** 50, 97, 119, 132; **Neil Holmes/Garden Picture Library** 66; **Clive Nichols** 7 (Arrow Cottage Herefordshire); **Howard Rice/Garden Picture Library** 137, 140; **Brigitte Thomas/Garden Picture Library** 116; **Steve Wooster** 1, 2, 3, 6, 8-9 (The Beth Chatto Gardens), 10-11 (Ethridge Gardens, Timaru, New Zealand/ Design: Nan Raymond), 12, 13 (Bowles & Wyer Design), 15, 17 (Ram House, Ireland), 18 (Glenveagh, Ireland), 19 (Ian Fryer's Garden, Christchurch, New Zealand), 20-21 (Ayrlies, New Zealand), 30–31 (Great Dixter), 33 (The Beth Chatto Gardens), 38 (Great Dixter), 39, 40-41 (Green Farm Plants/Design: Piet Oudolf), 42-43, 47, 48, 49, 52-52, 54, 55, 57, 59, 60, 61, 62-63, 63, 64, 64-65, 67, 68, 69, 70, 70–71, 72, 73, 74, 75, 76-77, 77, 78, 79, 80, 81, 82, 83, 84, 84-85, 86, 87, 88, 90, 91, 92, 93, 94, 95, 96, 97, 99, 100, 101(Ram House, Ireland), 102, 103, 104, 106, 107, 108, 109, 110, 111, 113, 114, 115, 117, 118, 120, 122, 123, 124, 125, 126, 127, 128, 129, 130, 131, 132–33, 134, 135, 136, 138, 139, 141.

A Zone Map of the U.S. and Canada

A plant's winter hardiness is critical in deciding whether it is suitable for your garden. The map above divides the United States and Canada into 11 climactic zones based on average minimum temperatures, as compiled by the U.S. Department of Agriculture. Find your zone and check the zone information in the plant directory to help you choose the plants most likely to flourish in your climate.

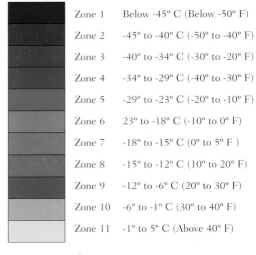

	Zone 1	Below -45° C (Below -50° F)
	Zone 2	-45° to -40° C (-50° to -40° F)
	Zone 3	-40° to -34° C (-30° to -20° F)
	Zone 4	-34° to -29° C (-40° to -30° F)
	Zone 5	-29° to -23° C (-20° to -10° F)
	Zone 6	23° to -18° C (-10° to 0° F)
	Zone 7	-18° to -15° C (0° to 5° F)
	Zone 8	-15° to -12° C (10° to 20° F)
	Zone 9	-12° to -6° C (20° to 30° F)
	Zone 10	-6° to -1° C (30° to 40° F)
	Zone 11	-1° to 5° C (Above 40° F)